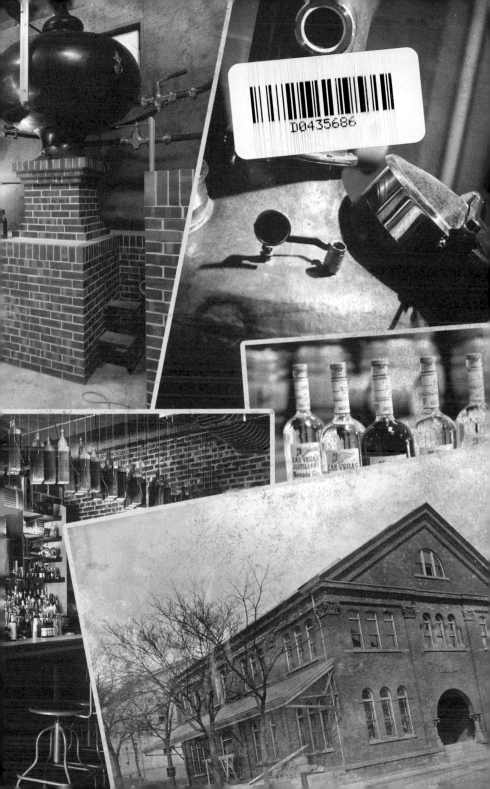

D0435686

AMERICAN SPIRIT

AN EXPLORATION OF THE AMERICAN SPIRIT CRAFT DISTILLING REVOLUTION

JAMES RODEWALD

STERLING EPICURE
New York

STERLING EPICURE
New York

An Imprint of Sterling Publishing
387 Park Avenue South
New York, NY 10016

© 2014 by James Rodewald

Interior designed by Yeon Kim

A complete list of picture credits appears on page 229.

ISBN 978-1-4549-0533-2

Library of Congress Cataloging-in-Publication Data

Rodewald, James.
  American spirit : an exploration of the craft distilling revolution / James
Rodewald.
    pages cm
  ISBN 978-1-4549-0533-2 (hardback)
  1. Distilleries--United States. 2. Liquors--United States. 3. Distilling
industries--United States. I. Title.
  HD9390.U62R59 2014
  338.4'7663500973--dc23

                                                        2014008401

Distributed in Canada by Sterling Publishing
^{c}/o Canadian Manda Group, 165 Dufferin Street
Toronto, Ontario, Canada M6K 3H6
Distributed in the United Kingdom by GMC Distribution Services
Castle Place, 166 High Street, Lewes, East Sussex, England BN7 1XU
Distributed in Australia by Capricorn Link (Australia) Pty. Ltd.
P.O. Box 704, Windsor, NSW 2756, Australia

For information about custom editions, special sales, and premium and
corporate purchases, please contact Sterling Special Sales at 800-805-5489 or
specialsales@sterlingpublishing.com.

Manufactured in the United States of America

2 4 6 8 10 9 7 5 3 1

www.sterlingpublishing.com

For Marella—my wife, my best friend,
and my best reader.

CONTENTS

FOREWORD

When America was very young, running a still was an element of smart farming—grain distilled into spirit doesn't spoil, it's easier to transport, and it's worth more at the market than the raw materials that went into it could ever be. Most of the early settlers came from nations with traditions of distilling—the Finns, the Germans, the Scotch Irish (The Scotch Irish!)—and they got right to work cranking out rough spirit a barrel or two at a time. Hyper-local, small-scale distilling was the norm.

Alexander Hamilton tried to get all the distillers to pay tax, but it didn't really work. Mostly, the tax was simply ignored. It seems that it was really hard to convince someone to get on a horse and go around asking his neighbors to pay money (which they didn't have) for making spirits (which they'd always done) to something they couldn't see (the Feds). It wasn't a very popular idea.

During the halcyon decade that kicked off with Thomas Jefferson's repeal of the excise tax on whiskey, in 1802, before the debts incurred during the war of 1812 made those taxes necessary again, there were about 14,000 distilleries in America. Most of them made tiny amounts of booze.

Consolidation came with the dawning industrial age, and the burden of coming up with the cash to cover excise taxes contributed to the steady decline in the number of Americans making ardent spirits. In the years immediately before Prohibition, the number of American distilleries had dwindled into the hundreds. Still, there were hundreds. After Prohibition, there were perhaps a dozen.

And that's where the industry stayed for decades. When I was a wide-eyed youth wandering the aisles of my grandfather's liquor store, most if not all of the American labels I saw on the shelves were produced by some iteration of the same distilleries that had successfully weathered the Noble Experiment. Of course there had been takeovers, buyouts, and name changes, but I would suggest that in this context (with a few exceptions) the changes were almost superfluous—just the shifts of big business doing business.

What's important to realize about the small group of industrial distillers that dominated the twentieth century is that they made (and those that are still in business still make) lots of different products. Today they spend a fair amount of time and money trying to make their products appear as if they were produced by the sorts of people who distilled things before Prohibition. They splash things on their labels like "From the Birthplace of American Whiskey" or "Secret Family Olde Time Recipe" or "Crafted with Care in Snake Hollow." (None of these are real; they are meant to suggest, not to accuse.) Some of these claims have a tiny grain of truth, but mostly they're marketing gimmicks. Although it looks as if the American spirits industry is comprised of many small businesses, each with its own label, it isn't true.

Twenty-five years ago, there were fewer Americans distilling spirits on a small scale than there were Americans milking their own yard cows and chopping down trees to build log cabins, which is to say, maybe three.

When I first started hanging around small distilleries, a couple of years before I met James Rodewald, there still weren't very many of them. The scene was growing; new ones were opening every week, all over the country, but you could still wrap your head around the entirety of the industry with a few web searches and two phone calls. It was easy to find the key players and the good products.

Then things started to change. More distilleries open every year, and the number of entrants to the industry is increasing dramatically. For example, a report by Michael Kinstlick shows that in 2000, five small distillers entered the industry; in 2005, fifteen; and in 2010, there were more than forty-five. I'd guess that in the fall of 2014 the number of small distillers in America hovers around 450.

Small-scale distilling resonates with our current cultural interest in authenticity and craft, and it seems to satisfy a desire, among a certain segment of our population, to work at something that isn't abstract, to actually make something.

While their predecessors, the craft brewers, had the advantage of producing something that was distinct and more flavorful than what Big Beer had offered, the distillers had no such edge. For the truth of the matter is that even if the industrial distillers might not have been exactly square about what they were making—it wasn't distilled six times according to an old family recipe from the birthplace of American whiskey, in other words—it was delicious. Even if everything on the label should be understood as no more truthful than the claims made by Clark Stanley for his Snake Oil Liniment (The Strongest and Best Liniment Known for the Cure of All Pain and Lameness was touted as a cure for neuralgia, sciatica, and lumbago, among other things), it was still good. What was clear was that the small distillers had a chance to do something different. They could actually make little batches of liquor. These mavericks could reclaim an American tradition. They could work with farmers they knew, make something carefully and with intense attention, and sell it to people they also knew—people they might run into at the bank, at the farmers market, at the diner.

Many took this path—artisanal, careful, and transparent—but the industry was soon split. A whole segment of the burgeoning industry got to work simply rebottling something that had been made at a large-scale distiller and calling it their own.

The dispute between these two factions has been the key issue, the central hang-up, in the craft-distilling world. I have seen, and participated in, the arguments, sometimes heated, over what constitutes a craft distiller. It has been the core issue, year after year, at every gathering, judging, and conference I've attended. I've seen cuts and gibes among the makers, and I've sat at conference tables trying to figure out what, exactly, the industry as a whole is supposed to do about the fact that there are two distinctly different businesses lumped together under one tent.

This fight is still raging, and it rages on in these pages.

What James understands, and what he puts on the table here, is that transparency is the key. There are a few ways to get a good product going, and among the makers of the best stuff, there are rarely any lies about how what's in the bottle is getting there.

Craft distilling is a burgeoning, booming business, very difficult to track, and often hard to make sense of, but James has done just that. By presenting the characters in these pages so honestly and well, James has given us a vital tool in understanding what it is that we're looking at when we reach for a bottle or call for a cocktail. He hasn't made an encyclopedia (it would be outdated before it hit the shelves anyway); rather he's provided an education and delivered the tools consumers will need. Along the way, he's told some great stories about the business of turning grains and fruits into drinks.

MAX WATMAN
AUTHOR OF *Harvest: Field Notes from a Far-Flung Pursuit of Real Food*

INTRODUCTION

For most of a decade, I spent my days—and many of my nights—looking for great things to drink. Unlike most of my fellow travelers, I was getting paid, as drinks editor at *Gourmet* magazine, to turn people on to the best of what I discovered. I got to taste amazing vintage Champagnes, spectacular single malts, delicious cocktails, wild rums, ancient Armagnacs, incredible *saisons*—in short, I've been lucky enough to experience all manner of mind-blowing spirits, wines, and beers. But the best part by far was telling the world about it. I've always hated "boasticles"—articles that might, for example, crow about having sucked down the last drops on earth of some priceless whiskey that had been discovered after forty years under a rickhouse* staircase. I've had such things, but no matter how good they were, knowing that almost nobody else would get to try them took a lot of the fun out of it for me. In the same way, cocktail geeks on a mission to collect every version of some obscure pre-Prohibition concoction seem to be missing the point: at its best, alcohol is a wonderful social lubricant.

---

* This and other terms with which you may not be familiar will be found in the glossary at the back of the book.

This is probably why some of the most engaging story-tellers I've met have been distillers. I've never had to verify their tales, so I can't attest to their factual accuracy, but I know for certain that they are always true in the larger sense. Where do distillers get these great stories? Do they lead more interesting lives than the rest of us? Probably not: they do the same tasks day after day, the hours are long, and the work is hard. Their backgrounds run the gamut from former scientists to high-school dropouts. Many have traveled far and wide selling their spirits; others only rarely leave their hometown. But as a group they seem, compared to most people I have met in more than twenty-five years as a journalist, more open to the world, more engaged with it, more idealistic, more dedicated, and, okay, maybe just a little loopier.

When I set out to explore the world of craft distilling, I knew I would find some world-class tipples, but I didn't expect the people to be nearly as entertaining as the old-timers I've met from Kentucky and Scotland. I was wrong. Not only were they almost universally interesting and eloquent, they also were more forthcoming than I had any right to expect. Where most small-business owners might keep certain pieces of information close to the vest, craft distillers shared everything from business plans to recipes and techniques. This spirit of openness, along with a can-do attitude, an inspiring willingness to go up against the many layers of bureaucracy, the bravery to put everything on the line, the desire to make something tangible, and the belief in an even playing field, strikes me as quintessentially American.

The more I talked to craft distillers the more convinced I was that the single greatest advantage they have over their more industrial cousins—bigger than the flexibility that comes with being small, bigger than the ability to source special ingredients, bigger even than the seemingly unquenchable interest in artisanal products—is transparency. Craft distillers will never be able to compete with big producers on price, and we're already seeing labels designed to fool consumers into thinking that industrial products are coming from small, family-owned businesses. That deceptive practice is likely to continue. It's impossible to imagine that the already overburdened agency of the federal government that is tasked with regulating the booze business, the Alcohol and Tobacco Tax and Trade Bureau (TTB), would be willing or able to create labeling rules to help consumers easily determine who actually made the stuff they're drinking. The best advice I can give to anyone who wants to support true craft distillers is to make sure the label says "Distilled By" and not just "Produced By," "Bottled By," or "Made By." That's not a guarantee—people will lie, and Big Booze's lawyers and lobbyists will certainly figure out a way to get around even that rule if the craft market becomes big enough—but it's all we've got at the moment.

An encouraging development in the fight for transparency may have occurred in April 2013, when the American Craft Distillers Association was formed. Some of the best people in the industry are involved—Rory Donovan from Peach Street Distillery, Ralph Erenzo from Tuthilltown, Chip Tate from Balcones, and Tom Potter from New York Distilling Company—and I would be surprised and disappointed if they didn't develop some sort of voluntary labeling system to help consumers make better choices. One thing I'd love to see would be disclosure of whether purchased neutral grain spirit (NGS) was used in a product, not because I think there's something wrong with using purchased NGS, but because I'd like to know if the base of what I'm buying is industrial ethanol. I'd also like to see a category for blended whiskies. Some of the best whiskies being released by small spirits companies were actually distilled by large companies like Heaven Hill and LDI (now MGP Ingredients) some years ago and selected, blended, possibly aged or given a special wood treatment, and bottled by a little guy. In most cases, the result is something more interesting—or at least different—than anything the industrial producer would have put on the market. Blenders should take pride in what is an honorable and very old tradition. Though a few craft producers who buy whiskey don't make a secret of what they're doing, very few brag about it. (St. George's Breaking & Entering and everything from Big Bottom Whiskey are notable exceptions.) Not only would this be a more honest approach, it would make it easier for those craft producers who intend to transition from selling purchased spirits, with their particular flavor profiles, to products they actually make from grain to glass. Making the distinction clear seems like the best way to attract the right kinds of drinkers to your products, and to avoid alienating them down the road.

Despite the boom in craft spirits, there are serious issues confronting what is, after all, a very young industry. A number of people I talked to in the course of researching this book raised the parallels between craft distilling today and craft brewing in the early 1980s. There are some compelling similarities, but two significant differences jump out at me. The demand for more flavorful beer was a response to the sorry state of industrial brewing at the time. When your choices are Budweiser, Miller, or, for the hoity-toity, Michelob, a hoppy Sierra Nevada pale ale or a malty Anchor Steam offer a giant leap forward in flavor. It's a different situation on the spirit side, where there are any number of delicious gins, rums, whiskies, and liqueurs being made in industrial quantities. This presents a different sort of challenge to craft distillers than those faced by craft brewers at the same stage. The other obvious difference is that you can't (legally) distill at home in the United States. In 1978, President Jimmy Carter signed a bill deregulating the brewing of beer "for personal or family use, and not for sale." Carter probably gets too much credit for the craft-brewing boom, but there's no question that making it easier for homebrewers to experiment with ingredients and styles they weren't getting from commercial brewers also made it easier for brewpubs to sell more flavorful, less homogeneous beers. Another element that separates the two is that you can make beer at home that is every bit as good as what you get from even the best commercial craft brewers; the smaller the still, however, the less control you have over the process (plus, it's illegal). Even if a future politician were to add deregulation of home distilling to his platform, there's no way most of us would be able to come close to creating spirits at home as delicious as what's readily available in stores today.

As for the similarities, Michael Kinstlick, cofounder and CEO of Coppersea Distillery in New York's Hudson River Valley, has crunched the numbers, and his findings are fascinating. Setting the founding of craft brewing in 1961 and the founding of craft distilling in 1982, Kinstlick superimposes the number of entrants in each industry. Both begin to take off at about the twenty-five-year mark. Projecting the comparison forward, he predicts that the number of craft distillers will quadruple over the next ten years. Followers of the craft-beer explosion will recall that there was a shakeout in the late 1990s, which would suggest a downturn in the numbers of craft distillers around the end of this decade. That this is being talked about might well make it less likely to happen, but that assumes that newcomers to the industry can afford to pay attention to the lessons learned twenty years ago, the main one being that you've got to make a great product. The enthusiasm for something new eventually gives way to a more critical decision-making process. There may be a few more years of people buying up whatever the local distillery puts out, but if the deliciousness per dollar isn't there, that second bottle is going to stay on store shelves.

All of this makes it a great time to be interested in craft spirits, and the year I spent researching this book flew by in an instant. Still, I often found myself wishing I were doing this research five years from now. By then the whiskies that I saw being made and barreled will be mature, and the impact of continued changes in state laws will have opened the door to even more talented and passionate people. I hope you will feel some of the same curiosity and anticipation as you read the stories of a few of the people I met who have put everything they have into creating something authentic, something of lasting value, and something delicious.

The Barrel Barn at Garrison Brothers Distillery.

CHAPTER 1

UNEXPECTED
TEXAS

‹꧁꧂›

Dodging Smart car–size potholes, I meandered the industrial wasteland underneath the 17th Street bridge in Waco, Texas. There I found Chip Tate, president and head distiller at **BALCONES DISTILLING**, one of the country's best small spirits producers. Tate was working outside a shipping container full of barrels waiting to be filled. Within seconds of meeting him, these words came out of his mouth: "There are a great, great many 'craft' distillers who don't make s--t. If you buy whiskey from other distillers—finished whiskey—you didn't really make it. The government will allow you to say 'produced by' if you didn't make the whiskey, but not 'distilled by.' Good luck finding a person in a hundred who knows the difference. It sounds like the same thing."

The content of the statement wasn't a shock—lack of transparency is a major source of frustration among craft distillers, and it's particularly galling for those who make whiskey—but given how much Tate had going on at that moment (not to mention his Master of Divinity from Union Theological Society), the vehemence was striking. I soon learned that the day had been a roller-coaster ride, with a potential investor first dropping out and then seeming, maybe, to be back on board. Later, his wife, Nicky, pregnant with their second child, brought him a fast-food lunch, which he shared in the back of the family SUV with their two-year-old daughter, Charlotte. Not knowing whether this backer would come through made a typically hectic workday even more difficult, and the presence of a stranger in the car made it impossible for Tate to speak openly. Nicky would just have to wait for this bit of crucial information. For that matter, so would Chip. More than a year, in fact.

It would be nice to be able to say that such drama is unusual, but building a business with your bare hands is never without complications. When the thing you're making is highly flammable and somewhat toxic, the stakes are even higher. The two-thousand-square-foot building that houses Balcones's Willy Wonka setup just barely accommodates the machinery, most of which was built or refurbished by Tate. "We got this building on July 30, 2008. It took about eleven months to have the distillery ready—there were three of us then. We were going to get two stills going and then put on two other stills I built shortly thereafter. Here we are in 2012 and that hasn't happened yet."

In the first few years several things held up the planned expansion, among them the engineering challenges posed by the

OPPOSITE: Chip Tate, president and head distiller of Balcones Distilling in Waco, Texas.

small space, the economic hardship that stopping production to reframe the building would create, and the fact that the stills are heated with direct fire. "It already gets up close to one hundred degrees in here even with the air conditioning during the summer," says Tate, "so I don't think tripling the still capacity is going to help us out very much." But in January 2011, Tate was able to buy a 1923 fireproof storage building a few blocks away, where he's been storing barrels full of whiskey with plans to move the entire operation there in the first quarter of 2015. In the meantime, he's producing about five thousand bottles a month of his unique spirits, under less-than-ideal conditions. "The only reason we can make as much as we do here," he says, "is our narrow focus. If it doesn't need to be on the floor it comes off—it's kind of like working on a submarine. The engineering on this was a little difficult to figure out. It's down to the cubic inch, not just the square inch."

On the day I visited, Tate was having a bit of a battle with his equipment. The spirit wasn't responding as he expected, so he kept going back to taste the raw alcohol coming off the still, making adjustments to the temperature, and checking a few minutes later to see whether the tweaks had worked. He didn't seem worried, just very deeply engaged. Despite all the distractions and demands, Tate moved from scientist to artist to small business owner to public relations man and back with apparent ease.

The first Balcones release was Baby Blue, in September 2009. It became the first legal whiskey sold in Texas since Prohibition. There's really nothing like it, and not just because it's made from Hopi blue corn. That would be interesting enough, but what really impressed me was that despite being aged in

OPPOSITE: One of the handmade stills at Balcones.

small oak barrels the wood influence was not overwhelming. A number of craft whiskey makers, in an effort to more quickly bring color and flavor to their spirit so that they can get it to market faster, use small casks to increase the surface area of spirit exposed to wood (the standard in industrial whiskey making is fifty-three gallons; I've seen casks as small as five gallons being used). But almost every other small-cask-aged whiskey I've tasted is too woody for me. The tannins can be harsh, the flavors spiky and unbalanced. The Baby Blue, however, is comparatively subtle. The fine tannins give it a lovely texture, there's a touch of sweetness, and its long finish is evocative of corn tortillas. I'm not sure that it's a bottle I'd go back to every day, but it is by no means a novelty; this is an extremely well-made and well-aged spirit. How does he do it?

"We're trying to make our corn whiskey really taste like corn, so we make it more like wine," says Tate. "We start with a very difficult to grow but very flavorful corn. We roast it to bring out the flavor. We do a very intensive mash and a long, slow fermentation. That's one of the most distinctive things. A typical distillery fermentation is more like seventy hours. Ours is seven days."

That slower fermentation creates a cleaner and richer distillate. Of course the longer something takes to make, the more expensive it is. This is compounded at Balcones, where the stills are used not just for distilling but also for mashing and fermentation. If they're fermenting, they're not distilling. And vice versa. The move to the new building will allow them to add

CRYING OVER SPILLED SPIRIT

I saw the ability to juggle multiple inputs in several of the best distillers I met; switching quickly between tasks is an important skill in spirit making. The one nearly catastrophic failure I saw came a few months after my trip to Waco when I was talking to a very experienced and highly regarded distiller as he monitored grain going into a wash tun, listened to his steam boiler (which he'd just turned down), and filled barrels with his white whiskey. He'd probably done this exact set of jobs simultaneously thousands of times. But he was also talking to me, so rather than being able to go back and forth between mechanical tasks, he was being asked to maintain a conversation. When I heard a new sound—the picture in my head was of a babbling brook—I turned, and before I could say what I was thinking, he sprinted across the brewing deck, dodged a fermenter, stutter-stepped some hoses, and leapt over the railing, swearing like a sailor the whole way. The flow of clear liquid over the top of the barrel was quickly stopped, and a glance around revealed perhaps two gallons of spirit on the floor. The swearing soon stopped and a thorough cleanup was undertaken. I still lament the loss—it smelled great—but my guilt at being the cause of the mishap is somewhat tempered by the knowledge that it would have been a lot worse if I hadn't alerted him to his whiskey waterfall. Just to be clear, this did not happen at Balcones.

stills, but more importantly, they'll be able to install dedicated fermenters. The result will be a major increase in capacity. Tate projects that they'll "be able to do about a hundred times more than we're doing now. I know it sounds like a lot, but it's not. What we're doing now is very small. And yes, the market will bear that."

Most of a whiskey's flavor comes from wood aging. Balcones takes a different approach to aging than do other craft distillers. The extremely forthcoming Tate becomes somewhat reticent when discussing this aspect of the operation.

"It's similar to what you see in the finest Scotch distilleries, only with American rules. We're not supposed to use new, charred casks to make corn whiskey [as opposed to bourbon, which has to be aged in new, American oak casks]. But did you know that if I take one ounce of whiskey and pour it in a barrel and pour it back out five seconds later I've got a used cask? You can probably figure out what I mean by that."

One might presume from that hypothetical description that Balcones buys new, charred casks, "uses" them, and then stores its corn whiskey in them. Not that Tate said so. "We don't want to call our corn whiskey 'bourbon' because it doesn't taste like bourbon. We don't lie; we're working around the regulations. I'm making a corn whiskey from 100 percent corn that tastes like corn, and I call it corn whiskey. Sorry, I apologize for misleading the consumer in that way!"

Of course everyone else could do the same, and some probably do. But Balcones's corn whiskey seems to benefit more from its time in wood than do other aged corn whiskies I've tried. As every baseball player, carpenter, and whittler knows, not all

OPPOSITE: Balcones uses small barrels for aging its whiskies, but constant monitoring keeps them from tasting too woody.

wood is created equal. Winemakers brag endlessly about their careful oak selection; spirits are much higher in alcohol, and most are in cask longer before bottling than wines, so they'll extract more flavor compounds. You'd think spirits producers would be even more concerned with this aspect of their operations, but surprisingly few brought it up or had much to say when asked about their preferred wood sources. Though Tate wouldn't be specific, there was no question he'd given it a lot of thought.

"We don't talk about where we get our small barrels from. It's a very old source of wood. All of it is at least ten to twelve years old before it gets made into barrels. The most important part is that the wood isn't kiln-dried. If you just use kiln-dried wood you get wood tea. It's not the same thing as letting the wood yard-age for three years. It's getting wet and drying, getting wet and drying. There's a lot of fungal action going on, and that's breaking down the structure of the wood. The water's

washing away a lot of the harsher tannins. We also use fine-grain wood, which is expensive."

Another unique aspect of the Balcones aging process is that Tate uses a combination of barrel sizes, moving the spirits into larger or smaller casks based on what he thinks the whiskey needs. This requires constant evaluation. Many of the distillers I visited had a few glasses holding barrel samples out on their desk, but Tate's tasting table looked like some kind of bizarre board game. I counted sixty-seven glasses lined up in a formation I was unable to decode.

"The typical approach to whiskey," Tate says, "is like this: Take a bunch of five-year-olds and lock them in the library for six years. Six years later you come back and a lot of them are fairly well educated. It takes a lot more effort and a lot more money to work with each individual. But if you're willing to do that, you can get much quicker progress. It's very time intensive to work that way, but it can be done. You also have to be good at predicting where things are going to go based on what they're doing."

The speed at which flavors are extracted in small barrels makes this attention especially critical. It's not just that there's more surface area of wood relative to the volume of liquid; it's also that the smaller volume of liquid heats up and cools down more quickly. That matters because temperature variation is one of the main forces acting to move the liquid around the barrel and into the wood. At this early stage in craft distilling, quite a lot of experimentation is going on, much of it driven by financial pressures rather than quality concerns. Some critics and consumers like the flavors imparted by small barrels; others—and I count myself among the others—don't.

WHERE EVEN THE
PROBLEMS ARE BIGGER

Texas has been one of the worst places in the country to be a small distiller. Unlike New York, Colorado, and Washington, to name three of the more microdistillery-friendly states, until September 2013 Texas didn't allow distillers of any size to sell directly to their consumers. They all had to go through a distributor, and distributors, particularly large ones, are more concerned with volume than anything else. Balcones's yearly production is probably less than what either of the two large distributors that dominate the Texas market sells in a day. If a vodka brand becomes popular suddenly, more can be made (or bought) and bottled in a matter of days. But when the demand for an aged craft spirit goes up, it's not possible to instantly increase the supply. This explains why the "craft" distilling segment in Texas has been dominated by vodka, most of which is made from neutral grain spirit bought from an industrial supplier. (Where the "craft" is in this escapes me. I tried to get the icon of Texas distilling, the charismatic, wildly successful, and wonderfully named Tito Beveridge, to meet with me. I wanted to discuss with him how he produces more than two million gallons a year of vodka, what possible benefits an alembic still could provide to vodka, and which part of his operation justifies the word "handmade" on his label. But repeated attempts to set up a meeting failed.) There are, in addition to Balcones, a few Texas-based, whiskey-focused companies doing things the hard way—sourcing their grain, fermenting, distilling, aging, and bottling with care. It's a huge challenge.

"If you want to say most of the stuff made in small barrels is junk, I'm with you," says Tate. "But it's not because they're using small barrels. It's like any tool. If you use a Weedwhacker to clean your teeth you get bad results. That doesn't mean it's a bad tool. If you use the same wood in a small barrel that you use in a big barrel, you're going to get something on the order of fifteen times the extraction. You've got to restructure the tool."

And that's exactly what Tate is trying to do. He isn't looking for greater extraction of flavors from the wood. Rather he wants to create conditions that will result in some of the same effects that occur in big barrels over longer periods of time. To accomplish that, he approaches the problem from a different angle.

"It's an equation. It's the amount of activity per square inch as a ratio of how many gallons are connected to that amount of surface area. I wanted to change the constant: that is, to change what that square inch of oak does. How do you do that? We use very specific proprietary toast profiles to thermally degrade the structure of the wood." Tate declined to get more specific, and he definitely has something worth protecting; no other small production whiskies I tasted managed to stay on the elegant side of the wood extraction line.

Balcones Baby Blue is also illustrative of another issue confronting many of the craft distillers today: success complicates your life. Tate's goal was to make a world-class single malt whiskey. "That was the reason I founded the distillery," he says. "But it was delayed by other ideas I had, like the blue corn whiskey. I figured, I'll try it out and see how it goes. It exploded. So we were caught between a rock and a hard place. On the one hand we did want to make a blue corn whiskey, but we also wanted to make a malt. But we couldn't afford not to make the blue corn whiskey because we were selling it. Good problems are still problems."

It took another two years for Balcones to release that single malt. Just as the Baby Blue, though made from corn, is not bourbon, the single malt, which is made from the same grain as several iconic whiskies from Scotland, is not Scotch. (That grain is Golden Promise barley, a name that doesn't suggest that it was created, in 1967, by exposure to gamma rays.) Of course being made in Texas it can't be called Scotch anyway, but the differences are more than semantic.

The desire to do something and the ability to do it well aren't always enough. "It's tremendously harder for us than for Balvenie," says Tate. "They've got whiskies going back fifty, sixty years. Not only can I not have stuff that old because we haven't been around that long, I'm broke. I'm always broke. If it sounds like I envy somebody like David Stewart [Balvenie's malt master], absolutely. It's a challenge for a small distillery. It's a good business, but it's a hard business. It's like railroads. It's a good, worthy thing to do but the infrastructure and the time it takes . . ." Tate's voice trails off as his mind returns to the harsh economic realities.

This should be a great time for a successful craft distillery to attract investors. We're in the midst of a craft distilling boom, the interest in starting new businesses has never been greater, and there continues to be reluctance to invest in traditional financial markets. In fact, two of the most successful small distillers attracted corporate suitors in 2010: Tuthilltown's whiskey brands were acquired in June by W. Grant & Sons, and Stranahan's Colorado Whiskey was bought in December by Proximo, the owners of Jose Cuervo, among other brands. But Tate was wary of getting into bed with the wrong people. "We're trying to bring investors on in a very old-school way: you give me some money, and I will do things with it, and I will make you money in return. Apparently that's a very old-fashioned notion. What most of them want to do is buy a brand and leverage the equity—they want to sell out. I'm trying to get more into the game, not out of the game. The irony is that the type of company these people want to invest in—that is, with the drive, the talent, the all-in approach—you automatically have a problem because I want to stay in. The kind of people who start this with the intention to sell it, they don't have the same drive."

Balcones also inhabits an awkward stratum, somewhere between microfinance and Microsoft. Two weeks before my trip to Waco, Diageo, which owns Johnnie Walker, had announced it was investing more than $1.5 billion in its plants in response to increased demand for Scotch whisky. The few million Tate needed to ramp up his operation would have looked like a rounding error to Diageo's accountants. (Meanwhile, the owners of Chattanooga Whiskey successfully raised $11,427 on Kickstarter. Their goal is to bring the production of their spirits—which are currently made in Indiana, alongside several other "craft" whiskies—to Chattanooga.) The number of medium-size investors is small, and it's hard to imagine Tate in a corporate environment. And with a BA in philosophy from the College of William and Mary, he's self-aware enough to know this about himself.

"You can't have too many free thinkers in a big company," says Tate. "It becomes impossible to manage, and as soon as you can't manage a big company, you become ridiculously expensive and you go bankrupt. You've got to have a corporate strategy. The problem is that doesn't work for a craft distiller. What made the craft distiller the thing that you wanted to buy is that they don't do things that way. They put their balls on the table and say, 'This is the one, I'm telling you.' And every time they're right they get to go again. This is what worries me. Investment is the major hope and the major threat to craft distilling today."

It worries me, too. Balcones's spirits are unique, they're well made, and I find some of them delicious. It would be a shame for whiskey lovers—and indeed for anyone who likes the idea of people making things—if that's not a sustainable model.

GARRISON BROTHERS DISTILLERY was established in 2004, but it didn't release its first whiskey until shortly after Balcones came to market. The company's single-minded focus is bourbon, but its whiskey doesn't taste like anything coming out of Kentucky. A recent shift from fifteen-gallon to thirty-gallon barrels will probably change the flavor profile, but every release is different, something its customers don't seem to mind. As long as the bourbon continues to be aged in metal shipping containers under the Texas sun, however, it will likely be dominated by wood flavors. The shipping containers are opened every other day to allow air to circulate (and, presumably, so that the alcohol vapors can dissipate), but these are extreme conditions for aging whiskey.

Toward the end of a tour of the beautiful Hill Country distillery grounds with owner Dan Garrison aboard a company ATV, I got a sense of just how precarious this business can be.

"I had a business partner," Garrison tells me. "I owned

60 percent of the business because it was my idea and it was my business plan, and the deal was he would provide 40 percent for the operations part of it. So I bought this ranch on my nickel, I built this building on my nickel, and I bought all the stills and all the equipment on my nickel. We were in Kentucky, and we met with Max Shapiro at Heaven Hill. [Heaven Hill has more bourbon in storage than any other company; it bottles several brands and also sells whiskey to other companies.] Max said, 'I don't know why you guys are doing all that work; I'll just sell you the bourbon. You can just put a Texas label on it, and you'll be rich by next year.' I looked over at my partner, and his pupils had turned to dollar signs."

Garrison parked the ATV back in its spot near the main building, turned off the ATV's engine, and pointed at the Garrison Brothers Distillery sign a few yards away. "That sign used to say Garrison Blank, with 'Blank' being where my partner's name was," he said. "I told my partner, 'Look, the business plan has always said, and the mission statement has always been, we're going to make our own bourbon—we're going to make the best bourbon in the world right here in Hye, Texas. You bought into the business plan, and you can't get out of the business plan. I'm not going to change my process; I'm not going to bring in tankers of Heaven Hill bourbon, already aged, and slap a Texas label on it and put 'Made in Texas' on it 'cause I think that's bulls--t and God won't let me do it and I won't do it.' And he said, 'We'll be rich; we'll be loaded.' We spent four months fighting. And one night down at the cabin—he was sleeping in the travel trailer and I was sleeping in the cabin—he walked in with a pistol and pointed it at my head. He said, 'Look, I've got $100,000 in this, and it's all my life savings, and I'm not going to let you ruin it for us.' I pushed him away; he was drunk as hell. And I got *my* gun out, and I said 'Get the hell off my property.' And he left. He held me hostage for four months. I paid him $250,000—$150,000 more than he originally invested. I was flat broke, and I had nothing left to do this with."

Garrison was having trouble getting the words out. He took a minute to compose himself before continuing. As we headed up toward the main building he resumed his story: "My brother and my dad came to visit. I was flat broke, and I'd put a For Sale sign on the business. I told them to come on up and check it out for the last time and taste the bourbon I'd made—this was in April 2008—and my brother and my dad loaned me $200,000."

He paused again.

"So they're the Brothers."

We'd made halting progress toward the building and had now arrived back at the front door. To the left of the door hangs a wooden cross flanked by a Harley-Davidson Motorcycles logo carved out of wood and a small cask protruding from the wall.

Garrison continued, "I got down on my knees before this cross, and I thanked the Lord. My wife invested; my friends invested. Today I can say I own 80 percent of this business, and my friends own 20 percent, and we're going to turn a million-dollar profit in 2014, and I'm going to give it all to my friends for their investment; and the next year we're going to turn a two-million-dollar profit, and I'm going to give it all to my friends; and the next year after that we're going to expand, and we're going to put in new cookers, and we're going to put in fermenters, and by that time this country is going to recognize how good this bourbon is. That's my dream. That's what I hope will happen."

RANGER CREEK BREWING & DISTILLING has found an alternative to the typical make-vodka-for-cash-flow, lay-down-whiskey-for-the-future approach of most small distilleries. Cofounders Mark McDavid and T.J. Miller still have their day jobs, in financial services marketing, and beer is their company's revenue stream. They also are releasing a series of small-barrel-aged whiskies while they wait for their straight bourbon to be ready.

San Antonio only allows alcohol manufacturing in areas zoned for heavy industry, which explains why the business is not, as McDavid says, "in a more visually appealing location." Yes, he is in charge of marketing. McDavid and head distiller Miller spend their weekends and evenings making whiskey. (Three employees take care of the beer side during regular business hours.)

"We're homebrewers who got cocky," McDavid says. "We were researching breweries, and we started seeing more and more about craft distilling. You read about Stranahan's and Tuthilltown and Anchor and Rogue, and you start getting excited. It's the front edge of this new, cool thing that's going to be just as big as craft brewing. Not only that, but we're in Texas, and making a bourbon in Texas just feels right. For a while we were flipping back and forth from being a brewery and being a distillery. We went up to Michigan Brewing Company [MBC closed in 2012], where Kris Berglund from Michigan State teaches a class

OPPOSITE: T.J. Miller, cofounder and head distiller at Ranger Creek Brewing & Distilling, in San Antonio, Texas.

in conjunction with still manufacturer Christian Carl. It's one of the few workshops where you can learn to distill legally. The brewery also had the still we were learning on, and we were like, holy s--t, how are they doing this? We talked to them in detail, and that's when things really started to click. It never felt right when we were talking about giving up one side because we were passionate about both. Then we started realizing we could really focus on the relationship between brewing and distilling."

One of the people who's been at this the longest, Tuthill-town's Ralph Erenzo, told me, "If you're building a brewery you're nuts not to add a still in there." The relationship goes beyond the simple fact that whiskey is essentially distilled beer that's been brewed without hops. There are a few hopped whiskies being made in the United States (and several German breweries make beer schnapps, which is unaged, distilled beer), but it's a tiny niche—and definitely an acquired taste. Some equipment, labor, and raw material can be shared, but the most important thing for the two businesses to share is fermenting knowledge. Another thing that can be shared, or rather passed down, is barrels. By law, a barrel can only be used once for bourbon; after that it will usually go to another spirits producer. (You see bourbon barrels all over Scotland, throughout Tequila, and wherever rum is aged.) But in recent years the practice of barrel-aging beer has become a bit of a trend among craft brewers. Ranger Creek has no trouble acquiring used barrels—every time it bottles a bourbon there's a fresh supply. New barrels are another story.

"We cannot grow our small-barrel program as fast as we want to because we can't get enough small barrels," says McDavid. "There are only three small-barrel manufacturers that I know of. I keep expecting to see more because this is a gold mine. There are all these whiskey distillery start-ups, and the guys we want to use as our primary barrel suppliers seem not to be able to keep up with even our demand. We did not identify that as a risk in our business plan."

Despite that challenge, Ranger Creek has released three small-barrel whiskies. The first was .36 Texas Bourbon Whiskey, maturing in medium-size barrels to be released as straight bourbon when it's ready (and when there's enough of it); the second, a mesquite-smoked single malt, is called Rimfire, and the most recent is .44 Texas Rye. Lovers of military history may recognize both .36 and Rimfire as types of ammunition with a Texas connection, the former being a staple of the Texas Rangers, the latter used in the Winchester "Yellow Boy," which was popular among frontiersmen. The .44 refers to the Colt revolver, which Texas legend Samuel H. Walker helped create, saving Sam Colt's business, which at the time was in bankruptcy. All three are part of what Ranger Creek calls its "Small Caliber" series, another in a long line of unholy alliances between alcohol and firearms. These whiskies have the woody flavors I associate with small-barrel aging, but they are clearly very well made and come close to being able to handle the woodiness.

Distiller T.J. Miller's explanation for using medium-size barrels for the straight whiskey, which will be the flagship spirit, shows just how challenging and stressful making bourbon in Texas can be: "We started off with fifty-three-gallon barrels. When we dumped the first couple of batches of small barrels, we had 20 to 25 percent evaporation. That scared the s--t out of us in terms of how that would translate to the big barrels. So we transferred them to twenty-fives. We believe, if you are going to work with the Texas climate, you'll probably have to use small barrels. From a production standpoint, and a cost standpoint, I long for the day we can do big barrels. It just takes so long. . . ."

But "long" is relative, of course. In Scotland, the minimum age to be labeled "Scotch" is three years, but you almost never see anything released that young. In fact, when the terrific Islay producer Ardbeg put out a product called "Very Young Ardbeg," it was a six-year-old.

"We're going to release our second product in our second year of business," says Miller, "and we're holding back. We have more ideas than we have money right now. If we had more fermentation space, we'd already have a second product out by now. We'll be pushing the innovation boundaries and giving whiskey drinkers new, interesting flavors. Kentucky products are high quality, but they're never going to release a mesquite-smoked whiskey. That's up to us. If we want whiskey drinkers to have a mesquite-smoked whiskey, we're going to have to do that."

This sounds a bit like what you might've heard from a craft brewer thirty years ago. In its earliest days, that industry was successful because enough people were looking for an alternative to cookie-cutter, largely flavorless, mass-produced beer (or, as Brooklyn Brewery's Garrett Oliver calls it, "beer-like product"). As Miller points out, "There are parallels made between craft brewing and craft distilling, but in craft brewing's case there were a lot of very similar tasting, unflavorful beers on the market at the time. Craft brewing was raising the game there. But when you're going up against Kentucky bourbon, that s--t's good. You've got a much bigger bar to cross. When you're coming out, everything you do is compared to Kentucky bourbon. People aren't tasting our stuff and going, 'Wow, this is way more flavorful than Bud Light,' or whatever. If we make a claim about being the best thing this side of the Mississippi, it better be pretty f--king good, especially for the price we're charging."

GREEN HELL

Courtesy of Elana Lepkowski
STIR AND STRAIN: A COCKTAIL SCRATCHPAD

1½ OZ. BALCONES BRIMSTONE CORN WHISKEY
1 OZ. CARPANO ANTICA SWEET VERMOUTH
½ OZ. GREEN CHARTREUSE
½ OZ. HUM LIQUEUR
2 DASHES REGAN'S ORANGE BITTERS
3-4 MINT LEAVES FOR GARNISH

Combine all ingredients except mint in a mixing glass filled with ice and stir until well chilled. Strain into a chilled cocktail glass. Garnish side of glass with mint leaves by dragging the bottom half of leaves through the drink and laying them on the inside of the glass so they look like little green flames.

The malthouse at Hillrock Estate Whiskey.

CHAPTER 2

ROCK STARS

TUTHILLTOWN SPIRITS is located in New York's mid-Hudson Valley, but the owner and founder Ralph Erenzo seems to spend as much time in Albany as he does eighty miles south at his distillery. Erenzo, who was a promoter of rock-climbing events around the country and ran climbing gyms in Manhattan, hatched a plan to create much-needed accommodations for rock climbers headed to the famed Shawangunks. In 2001, he found the perfect property for his "Bunks in the Gunks," and he paid $650,000 for a 220-year-old gristmill in Gardiner, New York. But resistance from neighbors, and two years of litigation, left him holding a very large, very empty bag, with no way to pay the bills. After selling off all but eight of the original thirty-six acres, Erenzo asked the local building inspector what kind of business would be less likely to expose him to continued local opposition. He suggested a winery, but Erenzo had reservations: there were already a lot of wineries in New York, and he just wasn't that interested in making wine. Then he heard about a new state law, signed in 2002, that created a distilling license category for production of no more than 35,000 gallons. The fee was only $1,450, as opposed to $50,000 for larger producers. Erenzo and his business partner, Brian Lee—whose MBA thesis was on microbreweries—received the first such license, in 2005. (In what might be seen as a final bit of nose-thumbing, Erenzo also opened up the property to climbers who wanted to camp on the property, free of charge, at his discretion.)

OPPOSITE: The tasting room at Tuthilltown Spirits, one of owner Ralph Erenzo's legislative achievements.

New York historically had been hugely dependent on agriculture, but cheap imports were killing local food production. That, according to Erenzo was one of the reasons a distillery appealed to them. "One of the incentives for us to get into this business," he says, "was to solve that problem. Brian and I saw farms being sold, apple orchards being sold, and farmers retiring. But then their four hundred or eight hundred acres gets turned into housing; there's no industrial base in the town, so everybody who has houses in the town ends up paying for the roads and the sewers and the fire protection and the schools that those houses require. And there's no farm anymore, so the place loses its character. Our thought was they just need something better to be selling. That's why we came up with the apple vodka and apple brandy idea. When we calculated it out, we could increase the value of the apples eightfold by turning them into brandy instead of turning them into regular cider or feeding the apples to the pigs."

Their first apple vodka, Heart of the Hudson, was one of my favorite craft spirits when I first tasted it, in 2007. At the time—and today, for that matter—apple vodka isn't what most people have in mind when they go to the liquor store. What people couldn't resist, however, were Tuthilltown's adorable half bottles of whiskey. I was excited to see a Hudson Valley bourbon, but when I finally got a taste I was somewhat disappointed. At the time, I'd never had a whiskey aged in small barrels, so I wasn't prepared for the overt woodiness. Others obviously felt differently, because everything Tuthilltown put out got bought as fast as the company could bottle it.

Erenzo is justifiably proud of what he's accomplished, and he can get a little prickly when questioned about some of the less traditional methods he uses (the small barrels, for example). "You have purists who will whine and moan and say something doesn't fit into the tradition, and I hear that all the time. I always say, 'Which tradition? Scotch whisky tradition? Irish whiskey tradition? American whiskey tradition? Bourbon tradition? Which one are you looking at?' The tradition

we follow is the American tradition of 'I can do that. I can figure this out, and I can make it work and make money out of it, and I can create jobs with it.' That's a real American thing. You hear it all the time. Some country asks, 'Who do we get to do this?' When nobody else will do something that needs to be done, the Americans always stand up and say, 'I'll do it.' We did it with the Panama Canal. There are a lot of examples of this, where the last best hope falls to the Americans who will try anything—because they

can, because that's the national character. People came over here and started with nothing. We're a perfect example. We shouldn't be where we are now. If we had followed the rules or followed the same history everybody else did, there's no way we'd be where we are now. The only reason we're here is because we thought we could do it, we set out to do it, and we did it. We didn't take no for an answer. That's a very American thing. You don't find that in Europe. Things are old there. They have long histories and traditions that we must not interrupt. Whereas here it's about saying, 'Hey, that emperor has no clothes.'"

It's also about playing the game, which is another thing Erenzo has become expert at. Even before he'd gotten over the initial stress of building the distillery, learning how to use the equipment, and trying to sell Tuthilltown's tiny production in a high-volume world, Erenzo was working on making New York State law more favorable to his business. The first issues he tackled were tastings and direct sales. Unlike wineries and breweries, distilleries were not permitted to offer samples or to sell directly to consumers who visited the facility. He lobbied for four years, saw then-governor George Pataki veto the bill twice before newly elected governor Eliot Spitzer signed it, and then had to wait for Spitzer's successor, David Paterson, to sign a slightly amended version of the law before a tasting room could be opened. (The New York State Liquor Authority, or "SLA," had narrowly interpreted the original law in such a way that Tuthilltown would have had to establish an entirely new business, build a separate distillery, and get a farm distiller's license in order to have a tasting room and to sell direct to consumers.)

"It's interesting work," says Erenzo, reflecting on all the time he's spent in the state and US capitals. "It's a shame it has to be done, but it's interesting to learn how laws get made and to actually get them done. Everybody gives up so soon on them. Everybody gets frustrated."

Ralph Erenzo does not give up. His former colleagues in the rock-climbing world know that, and so do his neighbors. Climbers are certainly among the most tenacious of athletes; after all, when holding on to a cliff by a fingernail there really is no other choice. That type of tenacity may have helped Erenzo in the days and weeks after December 21, 2010, when his Volkswagen hit a patch of ice and slammed into a maple tree, knocking it over and unearthing a large boulder. The engine ended up twenty feet from the wreckage. Erenzo ended up in the hospital for three months. His family essentially live-blogged the ordeal. Looking back at those web pages, from the early touch-and-go

BAR EXAM

Just about every distiller I talked to in the course of researching this book was, at one time or another, a lawbreaker. Though I suspect they'd all deny it under oath, when asked how they learned to make alcohol most indicated that their first experience running a still did not come after they'd received all their government paperwork. Perhaps this criminal behavior is what prepared them for the inevitable political negotiations that were in their futures. Not to diminish the interesting and often delicious innovations that craft distillers have come up with in the past two decades, their most important work has probably been legislative.

Eighty years after repeal, we're still digging our way out from under the post-Prohibition crazy quilt of state regulations governing the production, distribution, and consumption of alcohol. Some would-be distillers, in their quest for compliance, have found that their state has no mechanism for applying for a license. Others have found that permits are prohibitively expensive. And almost every state has treated distilleries differently than wineries or breweries, generally allowing the pouring of free samples and direct sales of beer and wine to the consumer while denying spirits producers those marketing and sales opportunities.

days through the "prayers for pee" (his kidney function was not good), the many operations at various hospitals, his first words ("I love my family")—two months after the accident—the upgrading of his condition from critical the following day, and the inevitable setbacks to the grueling rehab and triumphant homecoming, is as moving and heart-wrenching to read today as it was to follow at the time.

I don't know if any of the legislators Erenzo has lobbied or liquor authority officials he's debated have read the family's accounts of his recovery, but I suspect they wouldn't be surprised by any of it. He's clearly a formidable opponent, and he's probably accomplished more than most elected politicians. Erenzo doesn't gloat, however. He's seen attitudes change, and he's gracious enough to give credit where credit is due. "The last chairman [of the SLA] was a former state policeman. I went up there, and he told me, 'We consider you a legal drug dealer.' That's not the attitude to take if you want this industry to prosper and make money and create jobs. Up until now, if you called the SLA with a question, they'd say, 'You've got to hire a lawyer; we can't help you.' The governing legislation that enables the SLA to operate doesn't say anything about helping the industry develop, it only says 'regulate.' And they've taken that very literally. The SLA is now under the mandate to help the industry. They certainly appreciate the value to the state of the revenue, the jobs creation, and the contribution to agriculture and tourism."

The most recent Erenzo-led bill, signed into law in October 2012, gives farm distilleries the same access to farmers markets, state fairs, and county fairs as wineries and breweries have. Oddly enough, Tuthilltown already had that permit. "We were the only ones who even knew this other license existed. It was buried in *other miscellaneous permits*. Nobody tells you,

'Hey you can get a license for this.' You've got to find out. We were fortunate that in our visit with the chairman and the chief consul they said to us, 'You know, you can apply for this license.' Really, where do we find it? We dug into miscellaneous permits and found it there immediately. It does the same thing this law will do, but it specifically says that farm distilleries are allowed to get this permit. We put the law through the legislature because we wanted it to be part of the license. We wanted it to be clear to the farm distillers that they can go to these places. That'll be a big boon. Every place where there's wine set up, we can be."

Erenzo's legislative efforts certainly benefit Tuthilltown; when a law is created or changed, the distillery is in the best position to take advantage of it. But there's been an even greater impact on the industry as a whole. Thanks in large part to his efforts, New York has become one of the friendliest states for craft distillers.

"When we started there were six small distilleries in New York," Erenzo notes. "All of them were at wineries. Since we put product on shelves, in 2006, twenty-two new distilleries have opened up as farm distilleries. We can tell because the farm distillery license didn't exist before 2008. Four years, twenty-two new distilleries in the state. That's got to equal at least forty-five to fifty new jobs, and hundreds of thousands of dollars in excise tax and sales tax. The same goes for raw materials. We buy our grain locally." (As of June 2014 there were fifty-two farm distilleries in the state.)

You might think that Erenzo would now sit back and relax, having dodged the grim reaper, changed laws, and established a viable business. You'd be wrong. Erenzo recently turned his attention to some inconsistencies in the way American whiskey is treated in other countries and the way certain imports are treated here. "We're undergoing a struggle with the Scotch Whisky Association and the EU [European Union] because a few years back the EU changed the definition of whiskey to match what the Scotch Whisky Association wanted, which means it's a minimum of three years in oak, but it didn't say "new" and in American law there are specific exemptions for Scotch and Irish whiskies, but not for anybody else's whiskey. So, for instance, there are distillers in Wales and England right now who want to send their single malt whiskey over to the US, but they can't call it single malt whiskey because it's been aged in a used barrel and they're not exempt from the rule the way the Scottish and the Irish are. We can't use old barrels and call it single malt whiskey. So we've been struggling with the EU and the government to try to get them to designate American whiskey as American whiskey. The same way in our law Scotch is a Scottish product made under Scottish rules.

And Irish whiskey is the same. But they won't give us the same consideration, so we're struggling with that now. The better threat would be to say, 'Okay, quid pro quo, we want you to match the American rules then.' That would change it very fast. I've been teaming up with a fellow who's organizing a small-distiller's guild in the UK. I said to him, 'You guys have as much to gain out of the struggle as we do because if you help us get this law changed in the EU, we can help you on this side get the law broadened so that any non-Scotch or Irish whiskey can be in if it's made under the rules of that country. We have distillers in Sweden, Switzerland, and Germany, and they're all making whiskies, but they're aging them in used barrels, and they can't ship them to the US and call them rye whiskey or single malt whiskey.

"I'm saying, 'Your law's prejudiced against us, our law's prejudiced against you, let's fix them both at once.' You don't have to change the definition of EU whiskey. It can still be what the Scotch Whisky Association wants, but American whiskey is American whiskey, and you can't redefine it. It's an interesting struggle because in the beginning everyone said, 'No way.' But now we've got the international trade office and the US trade office, US Senator Charles Schumer's office is in on the fight. It wasn't a big deal five or six years ago, but now there are almost four hundred small distillers. There are only about eight of the big boys. Those four hundred distillers represent four hundred representatives and legislators and all their employees who vote. They're the ones they're going to listen to before the big guys who send their lawyers and lobbyists in to the legislature. All those big guys had old whiskey in

OPPOSITE: Filling a barrel at Tuthilltown Spirits.

their warehouses, so when the EU said, 'We're going to change the law to three years,' the big guys said, "fine." And the Bush administration didn't challenge it because there was no one to challenge it. But now there are four hundred of us, and we all represent quite a bit of tax money and a lot of jobs. So now we're getting the Feds to pay a little closer attention to the struggle. Because all those new distillers are going to be prevented from sending their legal American whiskey to the EU for three years after they open up, at a critical time when they need that market, and it's not right."

IRREGULATION

I've long been a fan of Japanese single malts, which are labeled as such on liquor store shelves in the United States. When I visited with Erenzo in the summer of 2012, I asked him how Japanese distillers were able to get away with calling their whiskies single malts since, presumably, they're not exempt from EU regulations. He acknowledged that the Japanese are using old barrels and that they are not exempt, but was not sure how they were getting around the laws. I suspect that the next time I see him he'll have an answer. And probably a new set of laws.

Somehow Erenzo also found time in 2010 to put together a deal with W. Grant & Sons, owners of Glennfiddich, Hendrick's, Stolichnaya, and many other brands, that transfers Tuthilltown's whiskey brands to the UK spirits giant. The immediate assumption was that Erenzo and Lee had sold the distillery, but they're still making a full line of spirits, including Grant's Hudson whiskies, in Gardiner. The astounding fact about this partnership, which the public does not seem to be aware of, is that the contract runs only until 2017. I've long wondered what Tuthilltown's whiskies would taste like if they were aged more slowly, in larger barrels, and it looks like I may soon get my wish.

"All the whiskey production is for Grant," explains Erenzo. "But we are experimenting, putting things away for longer periods. We're under obligation to them not to sell any whiskey to anybody but them until 2017. In 2017 we're finished with our contract, and then a lot of the goods that we're putting away now, which will be in larger barrels, will be five and six years old."

Other than the obvious infusion of capital, I wondered if the partnership has been beneficial to Tuthilltown. Erenzo didn't hesitate. "They've been helpful on the technical side and on the marketing side; they have resources we just don't have. Plus they have an international distribution system already set up. All we had to do was plug into it, and then increase production to meet the demand. That's a hard thing, because we don't want to turn into a factory. At the same time, it's not unreasonable to make fifty or sixty thousand gallons a year. That's not like the big guys, who are making that much in a month."

They're also working on new products, and Erenzo echoed Ansley Coale's philosophy (see Chapter 7) when describing his plans after the contract with Grant has ended. "By then we may have developed another product for them. We're coming out with our gin soon. Maybe they'll have an interest in that, or maybe someone else will. We've adopted the posture of an incubator for new ideas and new types of whiskey. Our goal is to build a product up, get it out there in the marketplace, and either keep it going or sell it to someone else if they want to take it and make it bigger. We're constantly looking for new things. We use different grains, or we use different strains of yeast, using rice instead of wheat—I'm sure somebody's doing it somewhere, but I haven't seen it. We think we can get something very interesting out of so-called Indian rice—natural, native, wild rice, grown in New York. Or oats. That produced a great whiskey. These aren't popular things yet, but with all the new distilleries coming on board, people are seeing the variety and learning to be more experimental."

Despite all evidence to the contrary, Erenzo says he's slowing down. Generally, when I tell people it's nice to see them I mean it, but I don't usually mean it the way I meant it when I said those words to Erenzo. His response indicated that he was well aware of what I was feeling. "It's nice to be seen! I don't take it for granted. I'm back on my bike again, and I'm swimming. I'm not climbing yet because parts of my toes were removed and I can't put a climbing shoe on my left foot. Yet. I have to move a little more slowly and carefully these days, but I'm moving! The accident had a great effect. I've relaxed a lot. I drive much slower now, and more conservatively. Everything I do is a little bit more deliberate. I don't forget for a moment that it's good to be alive."

OPPOSITE: The Hillrock distillery, in the picturesque Hudson Valley of New York State.

There's no clear definition of what makes a craft distiller. Some attempts lean on production volume; others focus on transforming raw materials into something not made by the large, industrial producers; others feel that if you don't make it, it's not craft, period. One man who's been on both sides is Dave Pickerell. He was the distiller at Maker's Mark for fourteen years, until leaving in April 2008; he now has his own business, Oak View Consulting, helping small whiskey makers realize their dreams. "I think there are three sets of craft," says Pickerell, "those that are making their own equipment, those that are making their own juice, and those that are taking something they bought and putting a spin on it—a blend or whatever—and bringing a new taste to market."

Pickerell's relatively expansive definition of craft fits his client base. Some are buying and bottling, others are hands-on at every stage from growing the grain to blending the final product. WhistlePig—one of the brands that often gets mentioned as being less than transparent about where it's made (Canada), although that information is clearly stated on the back label—is one of Pickerell's clients. (To be clear, I've never heard anybody say it's not a delicious rye.) WhistlePig is planning to build a distillery, but it has been battling a nearby organic berry and fruit farm, which is worried about the environmental impact a distillery might have on its property. Pickerell has also been consulting with Woodinville Whiskey Co. (see Chapter 9) from its inception. Woodinville chose not to buy already-distilled whiskey, preferring instead to make small amounts of vodka while pumping out and laying down as much whiskey as possible.

And then there's **HILLROCK ESTATE WHISKEY**, another one of Pickerell's clients. As the "estate" in the name implies, Hillrock grows the grain for the whiskey it's making. (What it's selling now, however, is largely "found," meaning bought, whiskey.) This may be a fourth level of craft: growing the raw material for distillation. Ralph Erenzo used to grow rye in a field next to the distillery and is now growing it on leased land. "The problem," says Erenzo, "is the necessity for a combine to harvest. Few farms in the East have one. The crop, nevertheless, is ours. The state of New York recognizes it as our crop on lands of our "farm operation." So technically it is our rye, but to use the term "estate" I think it needs to be grown on your own land." And the field next to the distillery? "It's now occupied in part by a solar array that generates three-phase power to make steam," says Erenzo. "We're trying to eliminate our dependence on propane."

Across the Hudson River from Tuthilltown, Hillrock is growing grain on its own property, and it's also growing on leased fields. "We've been growing grain for years," Pickerell says. "We started before we started building the distillery. Even on the leased fields, we're still growing it. It doesn't make sense to own all the land. In our area there are what I'll call 'gentleman farmers,' folks that own land but don't want to farm it, and they lease it out at very attractive rates. Given that condition, and given that we've now had a little success and everyone wants to be part of the deal, we can pick the field—which ones have been fallow, which ones are organically certifiable. We get the pick of the litter."

OPPOSITE: Hillrock Estate Distillery Solera Aged Bourbon Whiskey and Single Malt Whiskey.

The distillery is running seven days a week, and it may add a second shift at least a few days a week to increase production. What Hillrock does with some of the whiskey it's making is the most interesting thing about it. In order to address the difficulty that confronts a company that starts by buying whiskey with the goal of one day introducing its own product, Pickerell borrowed a technique called "solera" that's used for aging sherry, Madeira, brandy, rum, and even vinegar: Barrels are stacked in rows with the oldest liquid on the bottom. As the liquid is withdrawn from the bottom casks for bottling, the stock is replenished from the top down and left to marry and age. "We're the first in America, including the big guys, to ever do a solera," says Pickerell. "It gives us an amazing transition to our own product." And it is delicious. The high percentage of rye in the bourbon gives it spiciness and tones down the overt sweetness of many bourbons. Sherry casks contribute fruitcake, orange marmalade, and other spices. It's not a typical bourbon, let alone a typical craft whiskey, and with an $80 suggested retail price the consumer should expect something beyond the ordinary.

So it tastes good, but is it estate? Clearly not in any meaningful way, since the quantity of spirit made from estate-grown grain in the blend must be tiny at this point. On the other hand, the company isn't claiming it is an estate whiskey, though having the word so prominent on the label leads to the inescapable conclusion that they would like us to think it is. And there's no legal definition for the term in spirits, so even if they are happy to have consumers make the logical assumption, they're

OPPOSITE: To get its bourbon to market more quickly, Hillrock marries bought whiskey with spirit it has made.

certainly not violating any rules. That lack of definition doesn't just give Hillrock plenty of room for interpretation, it opens the door to pretty much everyone else. "It is a bit scary," says Pickerell. "It leaves room for somebody that's got no farmland at all to say, you know, 'Joe Blow's Estate Whiskey.' Anybody could say that they're an estate, and they could come up with their own definition. But I don't worry about everybody else and their claims. You've still got to make killer good-tasting stuff. I would rather rise and fall on the taste of my products. If somebody else wants to fill the air with BS, I'm kind of okay with it, as long as they're not lying."

In June 2013 Hillrock released its first product made from home-grown grain, an unpeated single malt (similar in style to Irish whiskey) that was aged for a year and a half in barrels ranging in size from just over a half gallon to fifty gallons. A "double-casked" rye came out in October 2013, and a peated

single malt and a Madeira-cask finished rye are both scheduled for release sometime in 2014.

Intriguingly, even when Hillrock stops buying whiskey for its solera bourbon, some of the found whiskey will always be part of any blend. As Pickerell says, "Theoretically there will always be molecules from the seed whiskey in there. As long as you don't pull more than half out at any one time there's always going to be molecules from every batch you ever made in there."

It's a very smart way to manage the transition. But as smart as Dave Pickerell is, and he's very smart, I'm sure he's not the first to think of using some version of solera on whiskey. It's still a time-consuming and expensive prospect, and definitely more expensive than simply buying a tanker truck of Kentucky bourbon, cutting it with local water, bottling it, and slapping a label on it. You're building a brand while you wait to have your own whiskey, right? "People that start with third-party stuff," says Pickerell, "[find that] the profit margin is pretty big if you can make it work. But there's an issue because that means you've got to keep buying. As you grow, you keep taking your profit and rolling it into buying more and rolling it into buying more. The theory people go under is, 'We're gonna take the profits and roll it into our own stuff and then do the transition.' Most people never get there because after two or three years they realize that the profit margin is great where they are. And as long as the found whiskey doesn't run out, they're in tall cotton."

That, though, is a very big "if." I heard this from others familiar with the available inventories of large American whiskey producers, and it was confirmed by Pickerell, who as a big buyer of whiskey for his clients is certainly in a position to know how the supply of available aged whiskey is holding up: "Right now the stocks are depleting," he says. "There's no rye. If you want rye over two and a half years old, you're out of luck. And there's hardly any bourbon left, and what is left, the prices are running through the roof. So the guys that are depending on third-party stuff, they're getting ready to run into problems."

If successful and well-regarded brands like Templeton, High West, and even WhistlePig are around in five years it will mean they either bought a lot of great whiskey early on or they somehow managed to make the switch to their own product. One thing that Pickerell doesn't see happening is big companies coming in and buying them out. This is another area where craft distilling is quite different than craft brewing was at the same stage: craft brewers weren't buying someone else's beer and relabeling it. "There's a massive risk for the buyer," says Pickerell. "They'd be hoping that whiskey supply endures, but what's to say somebody else won't come in and undercut you or that the supply won't dry up? Or, for that matter, why should we buy your company when we could buy the juice ourselves? I can't think of a single company that operates under the craft auspices that's 100 percent found whiskey that's ever been bought. And I'm not sure it'll happen."

George Rácz of Las Vegas Distillery.

CHAPTER 3

MR. LUCKY

eorge Rácz has got to be the luckiest man in Las Vegas. Maybe in the world. In a one-hour conversation, he used some variation of the word "luck" about himself twenty-four times. And this despite the fact that his business, **LAS VEGAS DISTILLERY**, was at that very moment hanging by a thread. Before we get there, however, how does a Transylvanian by way of New York City end up in Vegas? It may not be any stranger than a top medical student studying film at Hunter College, in Manhattan, or having a movie in the Tribeca Film Festival. But it is undeniably strange that this person would end up building a distillery in perhaps the worst

place in the entire country to start a distillery. How did this happen? It could be that George Rácz is simply a force of nature. And also, as he'd be the first to say, very lucky. In 2002, Rácz (pronounced "rahts") moved to the United States from Budapest after meeting his wife online. Life in Hungary sounded pretty sweet. "I had a very happy life," he says in his magnificent Eastern European accent. "I was working for a sailboat building company. I built sailing boats for rich people on the Black Sea. I never had in mind to go anywhere, but I met my wife—she came to New York twenty years ago to study; she was born fifty miles from my hometown in Transylvania. She found me and we got married in New York, on the top of the Empire State Building. I've been very lucky in my life-- every time."

And the life he built in New York sounded pretty good. He and his wife, Katalin, had a house-painting business that was doing well; they bought a house in Queens and had a son. As Rácz says, they had a "very simple life. We thought we would die in that house. Forget it. Four months after we finished it this idea came. I never knew it was possible for a small guy to start a distillery. But my grandfather—he had a very small and very illegal still, like everybody in Transylvania—told me, 'George, manufacture something.' Back in Transylvania people always looked for things that were made in the USA. We came up with the idea on Friday, and on Saturday we went to Tuthilltown [see Chapter 2]. I remember that Gabe [Erenzo] was very nice. He showed us around. His father was talking to somebody. They are like superheroes to us. Those people established the whole distilling industry in New York State!"

OPPOSITE: Las Vegas Distillery's Seven Grain Whiskey at various stages, from left to right: new make, and after one, three, and six months in the barrel.

The lesson there might have been not to take career advice from your grandfather if he's a moonshiner, but that's not the message that got through. So in 2009 Rácz packed up his family and moved to Las Vegas. They arrived on a Monday and the following Monday he flew to Spokane, Washington, to attend Dry Fly Distilling's week-long workshop (see Chapter 5). Why did he choose Las Vegas, you might well ask? Rácz's logic is impeccable: that's where the drinkers are. "This market is very interesting," he says. "There are two million local people, but it is a forty-million-person market with all those who are visiting. For all the big brands it's a top five market. For Grey Goose, Absolut, Captain Morgan, everybody. I thought, very naively, I'm coming here as the first local distiller and all the doors will be open. No. We had a two-hundred-page business plan. I think we could've thrown out a hundred and ninety-nine and a half pages. What we wrote down and what we dreamed about never happened. Why? Because there were no laws in Nevada. Zero laws. After Prohibition, nobody came here to manufacture. It is a tourist destination, gambling, mining."

But Rácz is not a glass-half-empty kind of guy. He's not even a glass-half-full kind of guy; his glass is always overflowing. So, undaunted, he began to pursue the necessary state and local licenses. (The federal license was, comparatively, a breeze.) "When I went to the first gentleman he said to me, 'So George, what kind of beer will you make?' I said, 'Oh my goodness. No, we will make whiskey, bourbon.' 'Oh, you are not able to do that here. There are no laws, and this is the desert.' So we figured out very soon that you need a lot of nice people around you. It took a year and a half to open. We didn't have any income. No paycheck, no nothing. We are very lucky because we had a little money from our painting company, but we needed more. But in 2009, everything went down. The banks said, 'Ah, you're crazy.' Nobody gave us a penny, zero. We had one big lucky thing: in the statutes of Nevada, distilleries are defined as a supplier. So if it's a supplier, that means distilling can be something! So we started to talk locally, and we were very lucky because we changed a couple of laws."

In January 2011 the Las Vegas City Council created a new category for manufacturing of distilled spirits, thus making it possible to actually do the thing that Rácz had moved there to do two years earlier. Of course he recognized the value of being able to put on tastings at the distillery and to sell direct to consumers. So, like Ralph Erenzo at Tuthilltown, Rácz worked on a bill to make that possible statewide. Was he lucky? You bet he was.

"We were very lucky," he says, "because in 2011 it was a session. We put a bill together that allowed us to give tastings and sell from the distillery, which is fantastic. It went through the assembly, they voted okay. But it arrived on the senate floor only two days before the end of the session. Of course it wasn't the most important bill in the history of Nevada, which was six million dollars behind on its budget, so . . ." Maybe not so lucky there.

BOUTIQUE DISTILLERY, ARTISAN SPIRITS, GOURMET EXPERIENCE.
LAS VEGAS DISTILLERY

Not one to let the perfect be the enemy of the good, Rácz, without knowing exactly how he'd sell what he made, fired up his still. On April 1, 2011, the first legal spirit made in Nevada since before Prohibition began to flow. Because the legislature only meets every other year, the law Rácz helped get through the state assembly would not be voted on by the senate until 2013. With direct sales off the table, he turned to the only other option, a distributor. Las Vegas distributors are very protective of their turf, and very big. Three companies dominate the city: Southern Wine & Spirits, Wirtz Beverages, and Nevada Beverage Company. "In June [2011]," says Rácz, "we knew that we needed to wait two more years. How will we do it? We contacted Wirtz immediately. They embraced us, and at the beginning it went really, really well. But there were less and less sales. We were like, 'Okay, what do we need to do?' Of course we needed more money. So we needed to figure out something else. And they were very nice—all the laws protect the distribution companies in Nevada. We went to them and said, 'Please let us go, because we need to figure out something. It's not against anything, but we will die like this. We will not be able to survive.' And they said, 'George, we respect what you did, you are establishing a new industry, we love you, do whatever you want.' And they let us go, zero problem."

Now that was very lucky. Except, of course, that he now had no way to sell a thing, and it was still several months before the legislature would meet again. Not long after leaving Wirtz, some friends stopped by to visit. "Why are you so sad? Somebody died?" he recalls one of them asking. Rácz explained the situation and admitted that if he didn't figure something out soon he'd have to close the distillery. He didn't tell them that Katalin had pawned her jewelry to keep the doors open a little longer. "We sat down together," he says, "and the idea came—why can't our local friends do it? They never sold fruit or anything, but everybody knows a bartender or a restaurant owner, and all we have to say is, please give us a chance, try our spirits. So we are in this situation now. And the state was very nice. They allowed us to sublease a space in the distillery to the distribution company. They said, 'George this will be a little bit of paperwork. Already we have twenty-seven million e-mails from everybody saying that we can do it."

The company they established, Booze Brothers Beverage, sells only Las Vegas Distillery products, and because of the strict prohibition against producers owning any part of the distribution or retail tiers, Rácz is not a partner. But, of course, he wasn't satisfied. Direct sales can be a huge boon to a small distillery, and Rácz didn't want to wait for the laws to change. A bartender friend has now opened a liquor store called Half Full, next door to the distillery. Rácz has created something unprecedented, and he knows it. "Almost for the first time in the history of alcohol in America, almost below one roof you will have the three-tier system, locally. It's a crazy thing. None of this is against the big guys. Absolut or Grey Goose is not the competition for me. They are in a parallel dimension. And the reason this could happen is that the City of Henderson and the state—they needed this crazy, bad, struggling thing to show we are honest, and that we are here for the next hundred years. Now many, many doors are starting to open. I had almost one million dollars in the barrels and the tanks. I was looking for money, but for the bank this is not money. They can't do anything with it because they are not in the alcohol business. I have one million dollars in value that I created in seven months, and I couldn't bring any money in. I had possible angel investors, but I didn't want to kill the business in two days. They saw only money, and I said, f--k it, I will not do it. It was a very smart thing. The same bank that said no to us three years ago, Nevada State Bank, is helping us now. The bank didn't change its mind because we had more assets. They honor the character. For them this is a crazy business, and it's not a 100-percent-for-sure business, but they honor that kind of character that's not giving up. And this is America. And actually it's not completely true that we can't give tastings, because the City of Henderson told me, 'George, once a month, when you have a big event or when you launch a new product, we will give you a tasting permit. You can make cocktails. Because we love you, you are here doing something that nobody did before, so why not help you? You are still here.'" It may sound far-fetched that a city official would tell this bear of a man that he loves him, but that's the effect Rácz has on people.

Now that he's created systems and structures that will allow him to legally make and sell spirits (after a series of amendments, and with only two days to go in the 2013 session, Rácz's bill allowing tastings and direct sales passed), the stills are running, and his spirits are as unusual and smile-inducing as the man himself—and, of course, full of his secret ingredient: luck. When he started he had three main goals. One was to experiment with recipes. "We wanted to try to use local things," he says. "I know this is the desert, but we are very lucky. There are a lot of little orchards, and we have a partner, Winnemuca Farms, so the wheat and the corn is from Nevada. We have a Nevada vodka—it's 100 percent wheat vodka—the wheat whiskey is already in the tank, and there's also the Nevada bourbon. We are very lucky, because 2014 is the 150th anniversary of the founding of Nevada. It's such

OPPOSITE: Las Vegas Distillery uses local raw ingredients whenever possible.

crazy luck to come out with the first straight big barrel bourbon in 2014! The barrel that Mr. Sandoval, the governor, signed will be part of the big birthday celebration in Carson City.

"My wife bought a seven-grain bread in Trader Joe's. So the idea came: what the heck, it's good for bread, it has to be good for whiskey. The lucky number is 7 in Vegas, so we made a seven-grain. The gin uses the seven-grain base, plus the usual botanicals like organic juniper, angelica root, and cardamom. I wanted to use local herbs, so we go out and collect desert juniper. Also we have locally grown mint. Something nobody's doing, I put small pieces of prickly pear cactus leaf in 120-proof alcohol for one week. It extracts a lot of cucumber flavor. We'll use a couple of herbs and roots that are said to have an aphrodisiac effect. That's the gin."

The spirit of experimentation is what led to the creation of Rumskey. "We started to make a rum, and we had a batch of fermented seven-grain whiskey mash almost done. The idea came one night: Why not marry the two mashes? So we took the fermented molasses, and we put it together with the whiskey mash, and we distilled it two times. What came out is not a whiskey; it's not a rum. The Rumskey is like nothing else. The governor was here, and he bottled the first Rumskey. We knew it was not catastrophically bad. We wanted to have a special spirit for cocktails, something for Vegas. Of course, nobody knows where to put it on the shelves."

You know what's coming.

"We are very lucky: Vesper is one of the best bars, and they introduced a drink called 'Rumskey in the Hendertucky.' Everyone says if you live in Henderson you are a Hendertucky.

So they created the first home-grown cocktail on The Strip. I put the seed down in the ground and a big storm came. Okay, we put another seed. I will be older, but I hope I will be around thirty more years to see what grows."

Another philosophical goal is transparency. "We are showing everything we are doing," says Rácz. "We don't have any secrets, we don't have a secret lake below the distillery to use for fantastic water, we don't have secret recipes. You are invited to come volunteer your time if we are bottling. Besides an open door, what we are doing is open. I think it's wonderful. You can come in, touch it, smell it, do it. A lot of friends are making whiskey together, because it's fascinating to do it."

Finally, he wants to have a "traditional artisan distillery." What that means to Rácz is "no mixing, no outside spirits . . . everything has to be made here." Like almost every small distiller I spoke with, he's been approached by people looking to capitalize on the popularity of "local" products. "Many people have come to me," he says. "'Okay, George, I'll bring two tanks of neutral grain spirits and you bottle it, and it's made in Vegas.' I said, 'No, I'm not here to sell the name.' Of about fifty people who've come to me, forty were like this: let's do it, let's make money, good-bye. I'm not interested in making another Tito's Vodka. I'm interested in experimenting, struggling to figure out how to make some fantastic new liquor that's made here." Of course the temptation, particularly when things were looking grim, must have been great. "I said no every time," he says, "because if you have your integrity, if you want to be authentic, if you want to be part of this industry for the next twenty years and you want to shape this industry, like Tuthilltown and Dry Fly . . . I can afford to go bankrupt, but I can't afford to not be truthful."

THE HENDERTUCKY

Courtesy of Vesper Bar, Las Vegas

1½ OZ. RUMSKEY (OR ¾ OZ. WHITE RUM AND
   ¾ OZ. WHITE WHISKEY)

1 OZ. APEROL

½ OZ. HUM LIQUEUR

1 OZ. LIME JUICE

1 BARSPOON BLUEBERRY PRESERVES

2 DROPS RHUBARB BITTERS

1 EGG WHITE

Combine ingredients in a cocktail shaker and dry shake.
Fill shaker with ice and shake again. Fine strain into an ice-filled
highball glass. Garnish with a sprig of mint.

Santa Fe is a great place to be a high-end architect. Or at least it was until 2008. But after the economy collapsed, affecting even Santa Fe's relatively resilient real estate market, Colin Keegan asked himself, "Who needs a high-end architect?" Then he asked himself what else a high-end architect like him might do. His home, just north of Santa Fe, in the beautiful and lush Tesuque Valley, has about thirty apple trees, and in years when frost doesn't nip the fruit in the bud, Keegan makes cider and apple brandy. He's a by-the-book kind of guy, so he looked into the rules governing home distillation and found that it was "highly illegal to do in any way shape or form." So he stopped messing with it. But he didn't dump the brandy he'd already put in barrels (he told me he "forgot"). As a lover of single malt whiskey, Keegan has an appreciation of fine spirits, and he was surprised by how good the brandy he'd made tasted. So he spent several months traveling around the United States sampling various craft spirits, taking classes, and thinking about whether he could open a distillery. In June 2010 he decided to build **SANTA FE SPIRITS**. And that's when things got really interesting. It turns out that, like Nevada, New Mexico had no clear regulations for distillers.

Keegan initially planned to put the distillery in Tesuque, build a stunning tasting room with an amazing view, and sit back and watch the people pour in as they do at wineries all over the country. "We wanted to set up in the county," he says. "We figured it'd be a lot more affordable, a lot more fun, and a lot nicer for visits. But the county wouldn't have it. Alcohol is not allowed in the county. Because school buses drive on the same roads." Yes, that really was the reason they gave.

But Keegan is not confrontational. He'd spoken to owners of the only other distiller in the state, Don Quixote, and they'd said it would take two years to get the necessary permits. If Keegan had tried to fight the county, he might have won, but it would probably have delayed the process another two years. Instead he went where he was wanted, or at least where the reasons he wasn't wanted could be discussed. "We bought our building and, because the state of New Mexico wasn't quite sure what a distillery really was, they had us apply for a restaurant license. We got a restaurant license, and they said, 'You're missing this form, and you're missing that form.' I said, 'But I filled in all the forms you gave me.' They had contradictory statements to the Feds, and the Feds had contradictory statements to the state. For federal regulations you have to own a still so you can give them the number, and then you can get a license. But in the state of New Mexico you're not allowed to own a still."

As an architect Keegan had a bit of an advantage when it came time to renovate the building. And he was used to doing things by the book—something that's a lot easier to do when there *is* a book. "We sat around and figured out what we needed." he says. "We read all the rules and regulations. Then we invited our inspector and he said, 'Yes, you would pass inspection. But I don't have a box on my form, so I can't inspect you.' We wanted to do it right anyway, but we could have done anything. I'm a rule follower; I would rather have rules there. When

I applied for my state license, they said, 'Ask the owners of Don Quixote, because the guy who gave them their license has left, so we don't know what you need to do.'"

Somehow Keegan managed to jump through all the regulatory hoops, get the building finished (including the explosion-proof room the city required despite the German engineer's stamped drawings showing that there was no explosion hazard; this is why Santa Fe Spirits is also licensed as a garage, because it generates volatile fumes—you can't make this stuff up), and get his Christian Carl still up and running. In early 2012 they started making spirits.

I wasn't surprised to hear, as I traveled around talking to craft distillers, praise for the old-guard like St. George, Clear Creek, and Germain-Robin; for trailblazers like Tuthilltown and Dry Fly; and even for experimentalists like Corsair. But on two separate occasions distillers brought up Santa Fe Spirits as one worth checking out. This is all the more remarkable given the limited distribution (New Mexico, Colorado, Oregon, and Texas) for its five products: a white whiskey called Silver Coyote; Expedition vodka, which is made from purchased grain neutral spirit and redistilled once in their copper pot still; the apple brandy that got Keegan into this mess in the first place; a gin made with New Mexico botanicals, including sage, osha root, and cholla blossom; and Colkegan single malt whiskey, for which one-quarter of the barley is smoked over mesquite.

Keegan had one very big stroke of good luck in the form, oddly enough, of a deep-pocketed potential future competitor. Gerald Peters, who opened his first Santa Fe gallery in 1972 and has parlayed his earnings from art and real estate into a business empire that also includes banks, restaurants, and breweries, began to look into opening a distillery and quickly realized that the only way it would work in Santa Fe (or almost anywhere, in my opinion) was if he could have a tasting room. At the time that was not allowed in the state, so Peters lobbied to have the law changed. With the help of Keegan, who despite having only been in business for four months was a special witness, Peters's lobbyist was successful. The Santa Fe Spirits tasting room now generates 20 percent of the company's income.

The tasting room is nice, but to succeed in a three-tier world even the smallest distiller has to count on a distributor to sell to stores, restaurants, and bars. Santa Fe Spirits is represented by National, a huge company, and so far that arrangement seems to be working. Not that there haven't been issues, but Keegan is well aware of who is buttering National's bread. "I'm amazed at how distribution and marketing and sales works—I'm an architect," he says. "That's what I think is going to crush some of the small distillers. You've got to pay to play with the distributors. I talked to a guy in Texas. He was being very helpful. He basically said, 'You need to show us the numbers that you can sell in the state first.' But it's a chicken-and-egg situation. I said, 'You have no idea how much I've got invested in this. We will be here, we have a five-year plan, and we will do what you guide us to do.' He said, 'We're not here to guide you to sell. We deliver. Show us where we deliver to, guarantee that they will take it, give us a couple hundred accounts.'"

After just a few years Keegan is well on his way to creating a sustainable business and doing it the right way. But he's learned enough to know that his way isn't the only way. "There are three ways to start a distillery," he says. "One is to have a massive amount of money. You start with making a great whiskey, and you wait five years before you open your doors. That requires bigger balls than I've got, unfortunately. Another way is what I would call the middle ground, which is what we do. We came up with some other products to find out how the market works and generate a little cash flow while we're waiting for our whiskey to come out. The third one is to do what one of our competitors in New Mexico does, which is buy a great bourbon, put it in a bottle, and sell it."

STORMY ORCHARD

Courtesy of Edward Welsh, Terra at Four Seasons Resort Rancho Encantado, Santa Fe

1½ OZ. SANTA FE SPIRITS APPLE BRANDY

½ OZ. DOMAINE DE CANTON GINGER LIQUEUR

1 DASH BITTERS

SPLASH GRENADINE

Combine all ingredients in a rocks glass filled with ice. Top with soda, and garnish with lemon twist.

From left to right: Rachel Inman, Emily Walsh, Daniel Ruiz, and Elizabeth Cartozian at Clear Creek Distillery.

CHAPTER 4
FRUIT AND FIR

Growing up in the 1950s in Roseburg, Oregon, about 180 miles south of Portland, Steve McCarthy probably ate a fair amount of fruit cocktail. A decade later, on the other side of the country, I know I did. Given what I know now, I'm embarrassed to admit that I often picked around the pears. Embarrassed because it's possible that those pears were Bartletts from Oregon, and possibly even from McCarthy's family farm. In a sense, though, my finickiness may have helped turn McCarthy's **CLEAR CREEK DISTILLERY** into the producer of some of the world's best spirits.

A branch of McCarthy's family had been growing apples and pears in northern Oregon since 1909. Agriculture being an up-and-down business, over the years the orchards were lost

and bought back, and by the time McCarthy was an adult he wanted no part of the farming life. Instead he ran the small hunting- and gun-accessories business his father had established, and when his father decided he "wanted out," as McCarthy says, he bought it for a dollar. In the course of running that business—something he did extremely successfully— McCarthy spent a lot of time in

Europe, where he made a point of sampling the wide range of local libations. This led, inevitably, to an appreciation of fine wine, and that was the gateway to "an interest in everything else from Europe that I could eat or drink."

As McCarthy said at the American Distilling Institute's 2012 annual meeting, where he was the keynote speaker, "I came to appreciate that the people I met ate and drank only what they grew—what they had. Their genius was taking whatever they could grow and making something wonderful out of it. Poor land that could only support goats led to chèvre. Undrinkable ugni blanc wine led to Cognac. Small, crummy apples in Normandy led to calvados. And so on."

When McCarthy found out that the ethereal Poire William he sampled in Europe was made from the same variety of pear his family was growing back in Oregon under the name Bartlett, he put two and two together and got eau de vie. At the

OPPOSITE: Steve McCarthy, founder of Clear Creek Distillery, Portland, Oregon.

time, Bartletts were fetching about half what it cost to harvest them, and fruit cocktail was about the best use they were being put to. "That's how I got into all this," he said at the ADI meeting. "I set out to rescue the Bartlett pear market, save orchard farmland from development for tract homes, provide myself with a decent supply of good Poire William, which was impossible to get in Oregon at that time, and maybe make a buck or two."

Mind you, this was in the early 1980s, when craft distilling was not even a category. Two small distilleries were founded in 1982—St. George and Germain-Robin, both in northern California—but McCarthy, even if he was aware of them at the time, looked across the Atlantic for inspiration. He bought a still like those he saw in Europe, found an old warehouse in northwest Portland, secured a sufficient quantity of ripe pears, and, not knowing what would happen, got to fermenting. McCarthy exceeded his own expectations. Though he was sure it would take years to get it right, he encountered a very different dilemma. "My problem," he tells me, "was that my very first pear eau de vie was pretty damn good. I thought, 'Oh s--t, this is just going to be a laydown.' And it wasn't, although overall we made relatively few mistakes."

Though that initial success left McCarthy less daunted by the challenges of making a consistently delicious pear spirit, he quickly realized that Oregon's laws could jeopardize his commercial viability. "When I started, in '85, I couldn't sell to the walk-in public. I got that law passed in '87. I think I smoked it by the legislature and the governor. I had a very good lobbyist, who was an old friend of mine and a pro. He didn't work cheap, but he smiled and waltzed that thing through. We still had to

OPPOSITE: Steve McCarthy guarding some of Clear Creek Distillery's liquid assets.

go through the motions—we had hearings, we had a floor fight in one of the houses, and I had to beg the governor to sign it. He was an old friend. He was basically pulling my leg when he said, 'You know I'm going to have to veto this sucker.' He wouldn't have done that, but he made me do a dance."

The importance of being able to sell to the public is something that comes up in almost every conversation with craft distillers. In 1985, it was probably even more important than it is today. At that time there was no "craft" shelf in the local liquor store, no cocktails made from local ingredients on bar menus, and Clear Creek had no budget for advertising. As McCarthy says, "I was the only one in Oregon, in fact I was the only one in the Northwest. Other than Ansley Coale and Jörg Rupf on the West Coast, that was it for the whole damn country!" Of course he knew full well that foot traffic by itself wasn't going to create a viable business, so McCarthy decided to take his products to the people he thought would be most likely to understand them. This was well before the cocktail revival, which began to hit its stride in the early 2000s, so rather than head for the bar he barged into the kitchen.

"When I started out," he says, "our best friends were the chefs. I didn't tell them what to use our stuff for; they would've been insulted. I made that mistake once. The guy looked at me like I was a bug. And he wasn't even French. I realized then that the chefs know what they want."

Today, with cocktails increasingly popular and well-made spirits and liqueurs in greater demand than ever, bartenders have become more important to McCarthy's business. In 2007, Pegu Club's Audrey Saunders bought an astounding twenty-nine cases of Clear Creek Douglas fir eau de vie, using it that summer in a gimlet variant (see recipe, page 79). Nonetheless,

McCarthy still feels more of a connection to chefs and sommeliers than to bartenders. Talking about cocktails with Eric Asimov of *The New York Times*, also in 2007, McCarthy said, "We don't consciously sell to that market. We get these bright-eyed and bushy-tailed bartenders who've invented something, and that's great. Maybe I'm dead wrong, but I've sought out the fruit and gone to great lengths to insure their purity."

I suspect McCarthy was trying to be provocative. After all, Clear Creek makes a spectacular line of liqueurs, and they couldn't be better in cocktails. I'm particularly fond of the cherry, which, unlike so many overly sweet liqueurs, is actually delicious on its own. But any cocktail that calls for Cherry Heering—Blood and Sand, Remember the Maine, Singapore Sling, to name three—is even more delicious with Clear Creek's cherry liqueur. McCarthy says he resisted making liqueurs because, "most are cough medicine. They're all synthetic and terrible stuff. There's some real trash out there. We made them the way we wanted to make them."

The base of the cherry liqueur is his kirsch, which McCarthy says is an extremely difficult eau de vie to get right. He uses ripe, crushed whole cherries ("the only thing that isn't in there is the green stems"), which are then fermented and distilled. For the liqueur, he takes his kirsch and dumps "a couple of tons" of crushed cherries into it and lets the maceration sit for six months.

I also love the cassis and the rich, juicy cranberry liqueur, which McCarthy explains is made from "fresh, whole cranberries from the Oregon coast, down near Port Orford. It's very good quality fruit. But no matter how much clout we have in the marketplace, and it's not a lot, you still have to sell these one at a time."

Clear Creek's eaux de vie are highly regarded and relatively well known, but they're still a hand-sell. After smelling the gorgeous fruit aromas, the first sip can be a bit of a shock. They are not sweet, but we've been conditioned to expect sugar when we smell ripe fruit. And they're all incredibly aromatic, complex, and very satisfying: a little goes a long way (another problem commercially—they're sort of the anti-vodka). McCarthy's pear eau de vie is spectacular, as are the kirschwasser and framboise, and the Douglas fir is the spirit of Christmas in a glass. If you love the smell of pine, you'll love the Doug fir. Of everything McCarthy makes, this is the one that seems best suited to cocktails and least suited to sipping (admittedly, pine is not my favorite flavor). It's the one product they push as a cocktail ingredient, although "push" may be a little strong. McCarthy says, "A lot of bartenders say, 'This is wonderful,' but it isn't something they've thought about using, so we do have some drink recipes for that."

McCarthy has thought a lot about how to market his spirits, and his resistance to trying to ride the cocktail gravy train is not reflective of a disdain for bartenders. In fact, he holds them in very high esteem. But he knows how the industry works and that he's competing for a piece of an increasingly fragmented attention span. "If you're in the vodka business or the gin business," McCarthy asks, "what's your job? It's cocktails. Same thing with rum. Those guys have got a recipe a week. If they have a new drink, they'll put eight hundred brand ambassadors in restaurants. Tomorrow! At noon. We can't compete with that. We're trying to define a niche for real artisan products that are super-high quality, that are expensive, and that really should be served neat most of the time. It's a classic corporate identity moment. What are we? Are we a maker of cocktail ingredients, in which case we might as well buy from Archer Daniels Midland (see box below), or are we an artisan distiller of stuff we think people should actually like to drink? Of course we're the second, but it's interesting how much pressure there is to go off-message and produce a handout with cocktails."

BETTER DRINKING THROUGH SCIENCE

Here's what Archer Daniels Midland's website says about its "Beverage Alcohol."

In a market where flavors are fashionable and tastes are trendy, alcohol beverage makers still come back to quality ingredients to create superior products.

ADM's beverage alcohols lead the way for cocktails with high quality, low impurities and clean flavor. They are odorless and colorless, which allows customers to upgrade or increase the alcohol content in beverages.

Citric acids adjust, accent and generally bring out the flavor in wines, cocktail mixes and spirits. And our high-fructose corn syrup and sorbitol perform for wine and flavored alcoholic beverage makers.

McCarthy makes everything he sells and is as critical as any of the distillers I talked to of those who hitch a ride on the craft train while buying grain neutral spirit from a company like ADM, which takes pride in processing sixty-six thousand metric tons of corn per *day*. (ADM says this is enough to make 99 million boxes of cornflakes.) His criticism extends to the Oregon Liquor Control Commission (OLCC) for its failure to allow only those distillers who make what they sell to sell to the public. "The language was," McCarthy says of the law allowing direct sales, "it only applied if the product was made on the distillery premises. Then the vodka guys and the gin guys eroded the meaning of 'made,' so you can buy a tanker truck–load of trash vodka and bring it here and put it in a bottle and do nothing to it, not even some token bulls--t, put a label on it and sell it to the public as a product made on the premises. That's because the OLCC is so weak. They looked at that issue maybe fifteen years ago when some guys were filtering vodka through lava rock and calling it Oregon vodka and making a ton of money. They're still doing it, though they're now calling it American vodka, so they're being more honest now. The OLCC didn't have the regulatory *cajones* to define what the law meant in clear language—which I wrote. They threw in the towel on day one. 'Made on the premises' basically has no meaning at all."

McCarthy distills several other things: from a single malt whiskey that's peaty enough to be reminiscent of an Islay Scotch to an aged apple brandy that might remind you of a calvados, though, as with all Clear Creek spirits, the aromatics are off the charts. Those two are probably a slightly easier sell than the eaux de vie. Presumably because his life is not difficult enough, McCarthy also makes six varietal grappas. I was shocked to hear that Clear Creek sells every bottle it makes—not because those grappas aren't great; they are—but because brandy made from the detritus of winemaking doesn't strike me as a commercial slam dunk in this country. As with the fruit he buys, however, he sources the pomace carefully. The muscat comes from Foris, the gewürztraminer from Tyee, and the nebbiolo—by far my favorite, mainly for it's incredibly long finish—from Cavatappi, a venerable Seattle winery that gets its grapes from Red Willow Vineyard, one of Washington State's best grape growers.

Given that he's got more than two dozen different bottlings on the market, it's a little surprising to hear McCarthy say, "I have to discipline myself not to get caught up in too many new products at the same time. In most cases we were the first to make this stuff here. We like to bring something new to the party and not just run around knocking off everybody else's whatever it is. Everyone's making knock-off Kahlua, knock-off Grand Marnier. If we grew coffee here, I'd be interested."

His restraint, and also his lack thereof, seems to be paying off. Sales in 2012, McCarthy says, were around $1.7 million, not a huge number in the liquor business, but pretty darn good for a craft distiller. From 1985 to 2000, Clear Creek had no growth at all, but in 2004 revenues started to increase significantly, going from $600,000 that year to $1.3 million in 2007. Like everyone but the biggest banks, its business took a dip in 2008, but since then things have continued to improve. It's incredibly hard for a company like Clear Creek to grow. Until you reach a certain size you can't afford to get bigger. (Of course, like most distilleries, the bulk of the company's assets are always liquid in the wrong way; when I visited in 2012, McCarthy told me he had $1.4 million tied up in inventory.)

"One of the things that kills little companies," says McCarthy, "is they can't afford a good bookkeeper, they can't afford a good lawyer, they sure as hell can't afford lobbying in the legislature, they can't afford paid advertising or professional help with PR. You've got to do it all yourself. We've done okay, but we now have a terrific part-time bookkeeper, and without her I'd be dead. I'm able to pay two salespeople a fairly decent base, but like all salespeople they've got a fairly big per-case kicker, so they're making real money, and that's the way it ought to be. I've got a terrific production vice president and a plant manager. They're well paid—they have to be, or I'd lose them." None of that would have been possible in the first fifteen years. But old habits die hard: McCarthy still picks up litter outside the building.

At the 2012 Good Food Awards, where the Clear Creek Poire William Eau de Vie won an award, McCarthy seized the opportunity to speak to his fellow craft distillers. He told them, as he recounted to me later, "If you want to make real artisan products you're going to have to buy raw materials. It's expensive. Let's assume you make a great product, you're going to need to get a good price for it to stay in business, and you can't do that without nomenclature. The success of Oregon wines or Walla Walla wines is based on the fact that if you pay forty-five bucks for an Oregon Pinot Noir, you know who made it and you know where the grapes were grown. With that kind of strict labeling you can support high prices—not universally, the market is not infinitely large. But if you do what [David] Adelsheim did or [David] Lett did or [Richard] Ponzi did, and you're straight as a pin, you will have a customer base that recognizes that and is loyal and is willing to pay what they have to pay.

"I've talked to smaller fine-wine distributors who are really our natural soul mates in this game, and I've had some very smart guys say to me, 'I'm not taking on any artisan spirits because we don't know what the hell that stuff is, we don't know who made it, we don't know where it came from, and we're not going to sell it.' For many, many years I had some very good distributors around this country where I was the only spirit in the house. And now with this explosion of little distilleries, some of these distributors are realizing they have to have more than just Clear Creek. Our labeling language is designed to mimic high-quality *appellation* in the wine world. So you know who made the stuff."

The best craft distillers are advocates of transparency. But of course that alone won't solve all the problems that present themselves to someone trying to make a sustainable business out of transforming great raw ingredients into great things to drink. McCarthy has boiled down his issues to four things. "You've got the basic technical problem—how do you make an eau de vie of pear? Well, I can tell you that in five minutes. The next issue is, how do you make a *lot* of pear eau de vie? We use half a million pounds of pears every year. How do you deal with issues of scale? I think we've done that. It's quite scaleable. We can just keep growing—we need space, but we don't think that there's a big difference in what you do as a little distillery and a big distillery. The third issue is business model: How do you run a company that depends largely on fresh fruit, that makes a weird product, that's expensive, and has the bottling issues in terms of scale? There is more of a scale issue there than there is in production. How do you put all that together and make some money. Finally, of course, how do you make distribution of spirits in this country work for you? The jury's still out on that one. We're doing okay, but it's amazingly hard work." (See Epilogue, page 211.)

After a few hours of discussing these issues with McCarthy it seems utterly insane that so many people are trying to follow in his footsteps. Comparing the efforts of the newcomers whose products I've had a chance to try to what McCarthy is doing, I'd have to say there's still a big gap. It will be fascinating to see what those who survive are producing thirty years from now, but without the European frame of reference, I wonder whether many will be able to come close to the purity and elegance of Clear Creek's eaux de vie. McCarthy seems inclined to agree. "I know an awful lot of people that make bad eau de vie. I don't know what to tell 'em, but I can't believe they're doing it. Are they not paying attention? Is it a fantasy? Are they role-playing? They need somebody to say, 'Don't bottle this s--t.' We've done pretty well at that. It is sort of a moral issue. At some point you need to grow up and say, sure this is handmade and it's artisan, but is it drinkable? The Oregon winemakers went through that in the beginning. About five years into it there was some incredibly bad stuff. You had a whole bunch of guys making it. A lot of them were people that shouldn't be in the wine business ever. Doctors. Doctors are especially bad."

DOUGLAS FIR GIMLET

Courtesy of Pegu Club (New York City)

1½ OZ. TANQUERAY GIN
¾ OZ. CLEAR CREEK DOUGLAS FIR EAU DE VIE
¾ OZ. FRESH LIME JUICE
½ OZ. SIMPLE SYRUP (SEE RECIPE BELOW)
½ OZ. HOMEMADE GRAPEFRUIT SYRUP (SEE RECIPE BELOW)

Measure all the ingredients into a cocktail shaker. Add ice, shake well, and strain into a chilled cocktail glass. Garnish with either a lime wheel or a sprig of pine (pesticide-free).

SIMPLE SYRUP

16 OZ. SUPERFINE SUGAR
18 OZ. WATER
1 TEASPOON VODKA

In a 1-quart covered jar or 1-liter soda bottle with cap combine superfine sugar and water. Cover, shake well, and let sit for two minutes. Shake again two more times or until sugar is dissolved and syrup is clear. Add vodka to preserve. Keeps in refrigerator three weeks.

GRAPEFRUIT SYRUP

16 OZ. SIMPLE SYRUP
1 GRAPEFRUIT
1 TEASPOON VODKA

In a 1-quart wide-mouth jar combine simple syrup and the zest of the entire grapefruit. Cover, shake well to agitate, and place in refrigerator for 24 hours. Pour through a fine strainer, pressing down on zest to extract flavor. Syrup will last in refrigerator for several weeks, but the flavor will dissipate over time. Add the vodka to preserve, and store in refrigerator.

Distiller Jay Settle checking distillation run on
Corsair's pot still in Nashville.

CHAPTER 5

GRAINS OF TRUTH

How do an associate professor of European Jewish history and the deputy press secretary at the Austrian embassy end up making all manner of odd and delicious whiskies, brandies, eaux de vie, and liqueurs? Practice? Just lucky? Yes, of course. But no, the real answer is one part family heritage and one part desire for a happier family. Sonat (pronounced "sonnet") Birnecker Hart and Robert Birnecker were living the dual-income dream, each spending far too much time commuting to their jobs from their home in Washington, DC, she an hour to Baltimore Hebrew University and he a half hour to the embassy. They were about to have their first child and were casting about for the life they really wanted. They

discussed restaurants and cafés, but ultimately they decided they wanted to make something. Robert's grandfather Robert Schmid is a distiller, and a good one, back in Austria, and that gave them a bit of an advantage. So they started to do the kind of research one expects from intelligent, well-educated, intellectual types. And yet, they went ahead and moved to Chicago and opened a distillery anyway. (If there is any justice, their firstborn, Lion, will grow up to be a Cub.) They call it **KOVAL**, Yiddish for "blacksmith" but also slang for "black sheep," in honor of Sonat's great-grandfather, who earned that nickname by leaving Vienna for Chicago in the early 1900s, and for Robert Schmid—"schmid" is German for "smith." That spirit of doing the unexpected and taking the difficult path because it's the right way to go is the guiding principle of Koval.

In Nashville, a similar question arises. How do an owner of a construction firm and an Internet entrepreneur end up making all manner of odd whiskies, brandies, eaux de vie, and liqueurs? In this case the answer starts as a tale of childhood friends making biofuel (as childhood friends do) and ends with them agreeing that distilling whiskey would be more fun. Unlike the Birneckers, Darek Bell, whose father, Ray, founded Bell and Associates Construction—now run by Darek and his brother, Brad—and Andrew Webber, who has started and sold various tech companies, have kept their day jobs, but they've hired equally smart, quirky, and creative people to man (and woman) their two distilleries—one in Bowling Green, Kentucky, the other in their hometown of Nashville—on the weekdays. Their company is called **CORSAIR**, a reference

OPPOSITE: Robert Birnecker and Sonat Birnecker Hart
of Koval, Chicago, Illinois.

to the fast-moving, hard-hitting, but officially sanctioned privateering swashbucklers who, unlike their completely lawless pirate cousins, hit only the enemies of the state, never raiding a ship strictly for booty.

Among the many things Koval and Corsair have in common is that they both opened in 2008, which is solidly in the second wave of craft distilling. At that time there were somewhere between fifty and sixty craft distillers in the country; today that number is roughly five times as high. They are also the two distilleries in America, and for that matter anywhere in the world, most likely to make a whiskey from a grain you've never heard of. But this is where they begin to diverge. Until March 2013 Koval distilled rye, wheat, oats, spelt, and millet, and released each of these in three expressions: unaged, aged in toasted oak, and aged in charred oak (which they call "Dark"). In an effort to simplify the product line and unify the packaging, the decision was made to focus on six whiskies: single-barrel bottlings of millet, oat, and rye whiskies; a single-barrel bourbon made with corn and millet; a single-barrel four-grain whiskey that has oat, barley, rye, and wheat in the mashbill; and an unaged rye. The unaged whiskies I tasted in November 2012 were elegant and perfumey, which came as no surprise: Robert was raised on eau de vie and, like Clear Creek (see Chapter 4), St. George (see Chapter 6), and Germain-Robin (see Chapter 7), he uses techniques traditional to European distillers and applies them to all manner of ingredients.

"I come from fruit distillation," Robert explains. "That's how I've been trained. The number one thing in fruit distillation, as it should be in most distillation, is you have your flavor compounds, which are responsible for bringing across the real flavor of the product you're distilling. Then you have other compounds, higher boiling compounds, that give it that bitterness, oiliness, and tartness but that completely overshadow the original flavor profile. Our goal is always to get the actual flavor of the product out. You can't do that once you put higher boiling compounds in there because you won't be able to taste the rye or the wheat."

The tradition Robert comes from is quite different than the aged-brandy techniques used in Cognac and Armagnac (see Chapter 7). For that matter it's quite unlike classic bourbon technique, where some of those higher boiling compounds, also called "fusel oils," are allowed to remain in the spirit with the knowledge that the years it will spend in oak will allow those more flavorful, and more toxic, compounds to be transformed by time, oxygen, and interaction with the wood. Koval's aged whiskies spend just one to two years in barrels no larger than 30 gallons (Kentucky bourbon is traditionally aged in 53-gallon, new American oak barrels; Cognac casks can be as large as 125 gallons and are reused) so proper distillation is crucial to avoiding off flavors and aromas. I particularly liked the Dark Rye and the Toasted Wheat, but everything I tried had a purity that was very appealing. Robert attributes this to the rigor of his cuts. This comes at a price, of course. "You have quite a loss," he says. "You make the cut, and you lose 20 percent more than other people who might

make that cut a lot later. So it's a much more expensive way to produce these products."

On the other side of the coin, the mad scientists at Corsair will ferment anything that can possibly be called a grain. From amaranth to quinoa, and everything in between, they've cooked it up. In fact, they recently released a tiny quantity of a twelve-grain bourbon. I don't think I can name twelve grains. Previously the most they'd packed into a single bottle was nine, a whiskey they dubbed "Grainiac," but they heard a rumor that someone was about to come out with a ten-grain bourbon. I don't know if that rumor involved Las Vegas Distillery (see Chapter 3), but when I was there I noticed a canister containing ten different grains to illustrate the proportions for a ten-grain whiskey. Of course, the people at Corsair did not want to be out-grained. The best defense being a good offense, they worked out a blend and labeled it "Insane in the Grain." There were only sixty-nine bottles released, so don't go running down to your corner liquor store in search of it. On the other hand, it's conceivable that Corsair has already cloned some obscure Egyptian seed and added it to their already expansive roster, so maybe you'll find "When It Grains It Pours" or "Grain and Bear It" on a shelf somewhere.

If whiskey made from every grain known to man doesn't provide enough variety for you, Corsair is also running spirit through its Bowling Green still with various smoked woods or hops in the Carter head, which is like a giant tea ball suspended in the pot still. The company is planning to try smoked herbs as well—smoked-sage whiskey anyone? Corsair is obviously not bogged down in tradition, and that makes for entertaining, if occasionally inconsistent, drinking. One thing it consistently does, however, is win awards. That may be in part a reflection of the sheer number of things they make and that they enter a lot of small, experimental batches in spirits competitions, but I counted twenty award winners out of twenty-seven products I could identify. That's a lot of awards, and they turn out to be a bit of a mixed blessing. They bring attention and provide marketing opportunities, but Clay Smith, the Bowling Green distillery manager, notes that "we won bourbon of the year for the nine-grain bourbon that we don't know if we're going to produce. Then we'll have something like our Old Punk, our aged pumpkin-spice moonshine. We did some experimentation with that, and then it wins an award right off the bat so it's like 'Oh yeah, we should probably get on that.' Luckily that was an easy-producer."

Koval has won plenty of awards, too, but it doesn't enter as many shows as do some of its fellow craft distillers. It is, however, one of the few to have entered the Destillata, which is the largest fruit spirits competition in Central Europe (where fruit spirits are serious business). In 1994, Jörg Rupf's pear eau de vie won best of show there, leading the judges to test the spirit for adulterants. When none were found, the award was given, and America was on the eau de vie map. Koval won a gold, a silver, and four bronze medals at the 2010 Destillata. Sonat prefers the European competitions because the judges are trained and the criteria are objective. "Robert has taken many spirits judging courses in Europe," she says. "They give you three versions of a brandy and ask which one has heads in it, which one has tails in it, which one is perfectly distilled. In Europe, and particularly the Destillata—which you can't enter unless you make everything yourself, grain to bottle, and you can't use additives or flavors—every judge has gone through rigorous training. They're not going, 'I like this better,' or 'I expect whiskey to taste like this.' They're trying to determine who has created the most flavorful, aromatic, cleanly distilled product. You get a gold if you do a great job. If you finish a race with a really good time, it's not about what color your tracksuit is."

It's also not a numbers game, but I was surprised to find out that Koval has made "thirty-five or thirty-six things," according to Robert. If nothing else, that's a lot of labels to get approved by the TTB. It's true, as Matt Strickland ("Brewer/ Distiller/Experiment Guy" at Corsair in Nashville) says, that "it's a little bit easier to get your portfolio up if you're doing eaux de vie and brandies. It's not quite as easy with whiskey, unfortunately, but we're working on it." Strickland really is working on it. He toils every day to make new and interesting spirits and says that "99 percent of the things I do the customers will never get to try." And you thought hitting a baseball was tough! Because both Illinois and Tennessee allow direct sales, Koval and Corsair can do small releases. Large distributors are not well equipped to hand-sell a few cases of some bizarre whiskey or eau de vie, no matter how spectacular, but it doesn't take long to run through a few cases out of the tasting room. This is the importance of direct sales and why it doesn't conflict with the three-tier system in place in most states: (1) a manufacturer can sell only to (2) a distributor, who sells to (3) retailers and bars. In states where direct sales are not allowed and all sales have to go through a distributor, experimentation and small production are practically impossible.

Chip Tate, owner and head distiller at Balcones (see Chapter 1) told the Lynchburg, Virginia, *News and Advance*:

"You can't afford experiments. An experiment means you make too little to release. So you've got to make enough the first go-round to actually release it, which means you'll probably go bankrupt if [it's not successful]. It's kind of like poker. You can't not bet. You can't bet small. You've gotta pick your hands, and you've gotta win." This may not apply to black sheep or privateers.

Several of Koval's brandies are produced in small quantities (by normal standards; maybe not so small by Corsair's standards). This is a very European practice. If a wild berry happens to be abundant, a distiller is very likely to make a batch of eau de vie out of it. "In Austria," Robert says, "they might make an asparagus brandy. It's made as a novelty. They can make fifty or sixty bottles, and once they're gone they're gone. Next week we're making sunchoke brandy. It's a way for us to showcase that we know how to do more than one thing, that we make unique spirits. On top of that, it gives us something to talk about: while you're trying the Young Walnut Liqueur you might try the Toasted Rye or the Four Grain."

Corsair's Darek Bell wrote a book called *Alt Whiskeys*, which contains more than sixty recipes, some of which his company has released. Others, like Cannabis Whiskey, it has not. Perhaps as a result of the inclusion of such an *alternative* alternative, the distillery gets some, well, alternative visitors. "Every so often we have people drop by looking kind of shady," says Clay Smith. "They want to show us their cannabis moonshine. I don't know if Darek's recipe ever got prototyped or not. He won't talk about it." As for whether such a thing might ever be commercially viable in states that legalize marijuana for recreational use, Smith says, "I don't think it'll ever happen in the liquor industry. The TTB shot down caffeine in beer, for

God's sake. We did look into doing a synthetic cannabinoid, but it's such a touchy area. We're still one of the leaders in experimentation, but at the same time, we like our license." Because they're not pirates; they're corsairs.

Both companies have found it useful, and perhaps necessary, to engage in additional commercial ventures to keep their businesses healthy. Koval has a separate company called Kothe Distilling Technologies, which is the US agent for the German stillmaker Kothe and also offers consulting services and puts on workshops for prospective craft distillers. A number of the distillers I talked to mentioned the lack of available training as a major problem in the industry, but—along with Dry Fly Distilling in Spokane, Washington—Koval is a notable exception. Though it's impossible to track the number precisely, Robert says that more than thirty of his clients have gone on to get their Federal license.

Corsair's primary supplementary revenue stream is contract distilling. While a company is waiting for approvals, equipment, additional funds, or any number of other necessities to come through, it can work with Corsair to get a product to market. Corsair continues to get inquiries, but the company is now in a position to be a bit picky. "I get calls every week from someone looking to contract with us," says Smith. "We don't want contracts, especially if you don't have any experience in the industry, because you don't know what's involved. You need to be as transparent as you can possibly be for us to even consider it. A guy from Texas wanted to buy our whiskey already aged. He wanted to take it in an aged format in barrels, redistill it, and put it back in barrels so he could say 'Made in Texas.' That clearly crosses a line."

SHUT UP AND MAKE SOMETHING

Corsair's Clay Smith has a somewhat alternative background himself, though he's less of an anomaly in craft distilling than he would be in almost any other business. He went to a school for fine arts, in Boston, where he also worked for a liquor distributor as a wine consultant. He moved to the University of Chicago to finish his degree, working for the university as a wine buyer as well, then to Dallas for a year, where he worked for a large retailer running its beer department. Shortly after moving back to his home state of Kentucky, he started building a still as part of an art project. When he met the Corsair principles, who'd only been selling for six months, he recognized kindred spirits. He also recognized that they already had a still, which meant he wouldn't have to build one of his own. Also, like the Birneckers, he liked the idea of making stuff. "My background was video and sculpture and installation," says Smith. "The way that this company was DIY from the beginning, coming from the biofuels side of things, was incredibly intriguing to me. I was smitten with the whole idea of it—the making of things, that tactile quality of doing something with your hands. I teach art for the university here, but I'm kind of over having shows. The University of Chicago is extremely heavily theory-based. There'd be grad students who wouldn't make anything and would talk for two hours in a critique. After a while I was like, 'Shut up and make something!' I kind of got burned out. Then this came along, and it satisfied the need to make something. And I can make a living at it, too."

WHITE DIAMONDS

Courtesy of Rhachel Shaw, Tradition, San Francisco

1½ OZ. KOVAL RYE WHITE WHISKEY

¾ OZ. COCCHI AMERICANO

½ OZ. LUXARDO MARASCHINO LIQUEUR

1 DASH BITTERMAN'S GRAPEFRUIT BITTERS

Stir over ice. Strain into a chilled coupe. Garnish with grapefruit peel.

As a company, Corsair is proud of making what it sells, and since word always seems to get around about who's making what for whom, it's smart to be protective of its reputation. Koval and Corsair are probably more dissimilar than they are alike, but they definitely share two of the characteristics I have found over and over again in the best craft distillers: integrity and transparency.

There is no manual for opening a craft distillery. Certain patterns emerge as you look at the ones that have started up in the last few years, but overall there are more differences than similarities. And that's as it should be. After all, the whole point of craft is to create something new, not to copy someone else. Anyone who wants to actually make spirits, however, has to be able to ferment, distill, and sell. Some people have successfully outsourced parts of the process, but there are economic and quality ramifications to doing so. A handful of distilleries offer workshops and classes to help people interested in exploring the science, art, and business of craft spirits. Two names came up time and time again: Koval and **DRY FLY DISTILLING**. (Downslope, in Centennial, Colorado, about a half hour south of Denver, offers classes as well, but it is one of the quirkier distillers, and though its class outline looks comprehensive, I'm not sure its methods are reproducible.)

The weeklong workshops offered by Dry Fly at the distillery in Spokane, Washington, provide hands-on experience as well as nuts-and-bolts advice based on the lessons learned by owners Don Poffenroth and Kent Fleischmann, fishing buddies (thus the name) who invested their individual retirement accounts to open their distillery in 2007. Dry Fly was the first distiller in Washington State since Prohibition, and it used that early-adopter status to its advantage. "We were able to set the game plan how we thought it should be, says Poffenroth. "We wanted Washington to be different from other states. We wanted to focus on things that grow here. We wanted to be long-term driven. We didn't want to have a state where we had a proliferation of people buying neutral grain spirit and going through a bottling process and labeling it 'Made in Washington.' We didn't want to dilute the meaning of those words. If we tell a consumer it's made in Washington, the consumer should expect that it's made in Washington."

Another advantage Dry Fly had that more recent arrivals don't have is that they were, at least initially, somewhat under the radar. (When their vodka won a double-gold medal and best of show at the 2009 San Francisco World Spirits Competition, they were on everyone's screen.) Today if a distiller lets it be known that he's going to make whiskey, the calls and e-mails start the next day; everyone wants to know when it's going to be ready. Dry Fly didn't make a drop of whiskey until almost six months after it opened. This might seem strange, given how long it takes for whiskey to mature, but they had good reason. "We made vodka the first six months," Poffenroth explains. "I wanted to understand how the equipment works. With whiskey, you're betting on something that's going to happen in the future. Until you've got the equipment dialed in, I don't know how you can make great decisions. You can consult your way into it, there's all sorts of people who'll take your money, but then you're consulting with someone else's palate, too, which is also not necessarily the greatest thing."

Both Poffenroth and Fleischmann left careers in marketing with corporate food companies, so the importance they place on the sales side isn't surprising. Poffenroth has responsibility for the production, though, so he's very tuned in to that side of the business as well. "You have people who want to get into the whiskey market who don't have the time, or didn't build the time into their business plan, to deal with real aging. That's why you've seen this proliferation of small-barrel, short-term aged whiskey that for the most part the industry

OPPOSITE: At Dry Fly Distilling in Spokane, Washington. From left to right: Patrick Donovan, head distiller; Don Poffenroth, co-owner; Kent Fleischmann, co-owner.

and definitely the media have rejected. They're putting things out early, or they're forced from a market standpoint to buy whiskey and blend it with what they're making. It's a survival thing. But ultimately it's not-great planning that led to that. It's a four- or five-year proposition. We're just getting to the point now where we actually have enough whiskey inventory where we can tell all of our distributors in all of our states that if you order whiskey we can ship it to you."

Because those market pressures weren't as strong at the time they started, they've been able to go slow and grow organically. Dry Fly is the only distillery I've come across that has been willing to put something on the market knowing it would run out before a new batch was ready. It seems like a strange strategy, but the reasoning makes sense. "We made product," says Poffenroth, "and we took it two-thirds of the way through its aging process before we decided if we were going to make any more. We wanted to make sure that what we were making was going to turn out like we wanted it to. Until it was most of the way through the aging process you really couldn't tell. We would introduce a whiskey and then we wouldn't have any more for a year because it took us that amount of time to make some more and get it aging. Rather than making a bunch of stuff and not knowing how it would turn out—that's an expensive proposition—we took that more methodical approach."

Poffenroth recognizes that things have changed dramatically in the short time since they opened. But even with all the real-world experience he communicates to consulting clients, a lot of them go on to open their own distilleries. Even some of the unrealistic ones probably go ahead, despite his best advice. "If someone says 'Our goal is to sell four thousand cases a year,'

I tell them, 'It's going to cost you $2 million to achieve that.' Nobody has the horsepower coming out of the gate to have that happen organically. What it costs to acquire a new customer rises every day because of the increased competition. And big producers are starting to take notice of the small manufacturers and trying to make themselves seem like they're craft, so that also makes it more difficult."

Dry Fly got Washington State's laws changed and opened the door for distilling there; the company makes excellent vodka, gin, and whiskey from Washington ingredients; but its greatest contribution to the drinking public may be the information and expertise it has shared with others. I suspect when the great shakeout comes, as it inevitably must, those who had the benefit of Poffenroth and Fleischmann's tutelage will have a higher survival rate than average.

The lab still at St. George Spirits

CHAPTER 6

GIVING VODKA A GOOD NAME

There are several parallels between Clear Creek Distillery (see Chapter 4) and **ST. GEORGE SPIRITS**, the main one being they were both founded to make eau de vie. There are also plenty of differences, the most striking of which is in the product line. Whereas Clear Creek's Steve McCarthy is wary of getting distracted by too many new products, St. George co-owner and master distiller (though his business card identifies him simply as "Evil Genius") Lance Winters will try anything. This may not always lead to commercially viable products, but it often leads to some pretty good war stories. And Winters spent eight years working as a nuclear engineer for the US Navy, so war stories have plenty of currency for him.

When Winters first came to St. George, in 1995, he had left the navy and was working at a brewpub in Hayward, California, about twenty miles southeast of the Alameda Naval Complex where he had been stationed (and, fittingly, where the distillery is located). Making beer got a lot more interesting for Winters when he realized that it was the precursor to whiskey. That led him to experimentation, the results of which he claims are still delicious nearly twenty years later. It also led him to the nearest distillery, St. George, then being run by the founder, Jörg Rupf, and his distiller, Bill Manshardt. At the time, they were making eau de vie, which Winters refers to facetiously as "a cash-flow machine." Most of the sales were to Europe, where there was actually a market for the product. But Rupf, who had been a judge in Germany before falling in love with the Bay Area in the 1970s, didn't have huge ambitions. "He was doing very little," says Winters, "and he didn't need to do much. He was a man of simple means. Then he started to grow a little bit, and that's when he hired Bill. Together they made really, really solidly good eau de vies. Bill was ready to retire when I wandered in through the door."

Despite coming from a long line of eau de vie distillers, Rupf obviously felt he could teach passionate amateurs to produce great spirits. He hired Winters to replace Manshardt. "Jörg taught me that eau de vie philosophy before I started making whiskey—before I started making whiskey legally," Winters says. "I'd been making it at home for a while. I had no idea why it was turning out as good as it was until I came here and learned more about distilling from Jörg. That philosophy is: embrace what you love about the raw material. When we approached whiskey, it was from an eau de vie maker's point of view. What's the raw material for whiskey? Well, it's beer. How do you make the best whiskey? You start with the best, most interesting beer you can."

At the time, just making a whiskey and putting it out in the market wasn't enough to guarantee sales. In fact, no matter how good it was, the likelihood of getting a buyer or bartender to try it was pretty slim. "Nobody was ready for a single malt that came from the United States," Winters recalls. "I'd hear, 'Wait, it's an American whiskey, and it's not a bourbon? How old is it?' Well, at that point it was three years old, so the next thing I'd hear would be, 'No, I don't want to try it.' Slowly people have warmed up to it to the point where now it's an allocated item for us."

Winters still loves making whiskey, and eau de vie continues to be extremely important to the company, but for much of the past decade St. George's meal ticket has been flavored vodka. Hangar One vodkas were born, according to Winters, out of his forays into the marketplace trying to sell their niche products. "We'd have a lot of slow periods at the distillery, and I'd use that time to go out and work with sales reps. I'm taking out eau de vie and taking out the whiskey, and I'm seeing all these vodkas that are taking off. I tried somebody's orange-flavored vodka, and I'm like, 'Whoa that stinks.' I came back to the distillery, and I said, 'Jörg, there's all these people out there, and they're selling the s--t out of this horrible product. The eau de vies that we make carry more flavor and more aroma. What if we just sort of said the same thing we're saying with the eau de vie and said it in vodka instead?' We started playing around with that and came up with Hangar One. Those took off for us. It was a much bigger volume thing than anything we'd ever seen."

Hangar One is made with purchased grain neutral spirit blended with St. George eau de vie. Is this a craft product? It has a much better claim than many marketed as such. Now that the brand has been purchased by Proximo, there's no way to know what the future holds. Whether Hangar One is now or ever was a craft product is less important, however, than what it has allowed Winters to do. Like Ansley Coale at Germain-Robin (see Chapter 7), the infusion of capital (by far the hardest infusion for craft distillers to make) has given Winters the freedom to pursue pretty much every idea that comes into the lab still that lives in his head without fear of sending the company into bankruptcy. And most of them work (apparently cantaloupe eau de vie remains elusive). To its credit, St. George has always been completely transparent about how it has made

OPPOSITE: Lance Winters, owner and master distiller of
St. George Spirits, Alameda, California.

Hangar One. While most vodka marketing depends heavily on dubious claims about the number of times the product has been distilled—dubious because, with just a handful of exceptions, vodka is made on a continuous still and not in batches in a pot still—here's what a piece of pre-Proximo Hangar One trade material says:

> **How many times is hangar one distilled?**
> **Twice:** once by the original manufacturer, once by St. George. We don't like this question, because almost all of the vodkas that claim they are distilled multiple times are misleading the consumer. Here's why—no one is putting vodka through a column (Coffey) still and then doing it again.

Perhaps not surprisingly, Proximo's Hangar One website makes frequent use of the word "craft" and almost completely omits the fact that the base of all the flavored vodkas is grain neutral spirit (a video with Rupf is the one exception I could find). They're still excellent products, particularly the Buddha's Hand. But as the craft distilling segment of the industry continues to grow, there will be more and more choices, and I'm convinced that transparency will be one of the key points of difference that determines consumer choice. Confronted with a few dozen citrus vodkas, a certain kind of drinker will be attracted to honest labeling and repelled by bogus claims. Determining which claims are bogus will be a continuing challenge, of course, but if one label explains why saying your vodka was distilled dozens of times is misleading, it might make a lot of the other vodkas look less appealing.

Repeated calls and e-mails to Tom Hogue, the director

of congressional and public affairs at the TTB, in an effort to determine how "times distilled" claims are evaluated, finally yielded a remarkably useless response (even for a government official): if a label claims multiple distillations, the claim has to be "truthful." Though I'd asked how the agency determines the truthfulness of such a claim when a spirit is made by continuous distillation, Hogue was unwilling or unable to answer the question. Several follow-ups went unanswered. I also asked a few distillers who make such claims, and the closest I could get to a justification was that by counting the number of "distillation points" it was possible to say how many times a spirit had been distilled.

Consultant Dave Pickerell (see Chapter 2), who's dealt with the TTB quite a lot over the years, defends the agency: "The TTB is far too short-staffed to investigate every claim for truthfulness. Generally speaking, all claims in the 'puffery' section of the label are approved." But he also agrees that multiple distillation numbers are very fuzzy. When a vodka is made using a batch process, the number of times it's run through the still would be a true reflection of how many times it was distilled. But it's not easy to get a spirit to 190 proof in a pot still (unless it has a column attached to it). There are those who say that each rectification plate in a column represents an opportunity for alcohol vapor to turn back into a liquid and that therefore each plate counts as a distillation. "Opportunity" seems like a bit of a weasel-word here; there doesn't seem to be any reason to believe that all the alcohol vapor running through a still will re-condense into a liquid at each "distillation point." Some column stills are divided into sections, each of which performs a specific type of distillation, and it could be said that each of these sections represents a distinct distillation. However, not all the vapor passes through each section, and the vapor doesn't re-condense in each section so it fails to meet the definition of a distillation. Finally, a large producer of grain neutral spirit might have a still with many columns, and the number of columns might be the basis for a multiple distillation number. However, as Pickerell points out, all the "product" does not pass through all the columns, and it is not "condensed to a liquid until the end of the whole train." The bottom line is that there's almost no way to know how many times a particular vodka is distilled, and even less evidence that more distillations correlates to a better vodka. There is one thing that is as clear as a 190-proof spirit: the consumer can determine very little from most spirit labels.

Winters, however, is obviously fully committed to truth in labeling. A good example is Breaking & Entering Bourbon. In case the name didn't tip you off, this is not a whiskey St. George made, it's one it went to Kentucky and pilfered. Actually, Winters and his assistant distiller, Dave Smith, visited a number of bourbon distilleries, tasted various casks, and bought nearly four hundred 53-gallon barrels of bourbon and brought them back to California to blend. Given the general disdain among craft distillers for those who buy rather than make what they're selling, this may seem like a surprising choice, but Winters explains that "there are a number of places that do that, and it does make me crazy. It's like if you had great notoriety as a chef in Texas and somebody walks into your kitchen and finds can after can of Hormel chili. What the f--k? What are you doing? The problem is they're trying to get cash flow and trying to be a relatively large viable business early on. Then they're going to create their house style, and they won't want to change it if it's working for them. A lot of consumers are going to be getting the wrong idea. We want to be guys that make stuff. When we decided to buy some bourbon, I was very specific about how I wanted this approached. I said, 'I don't want there to be any confusion in the marketplace as to what our role in this was.' We found this stuff at a number of rickhouses, we put it together in a way that no one else would put it together—a half dozen or so big distillers around Kentucky aren't going to call each other up and say, 'Hey, let's see what we can blend out of all of our stuff.' We call it Breaking & Entering so that people know that we stole it, and we package it dramatically differently from everything else we do. *Artisan distillers since 1982. Bourbon lifters since 2011.* Right on the label we let people know we didn't make this; we blended it."

All of which is certainly preferable to, say, creating a label with a Texas star, calling it "Sam Houston," and revealing in tiny type on the back that the whiskey was distilled in Kentucky. Or putting a huge TX on your bottle, a "Go Texan" seal on the back, and a blend of American whiskies inside. Not to pick on Texas (and not to imply that any of those products are in any way inferior), but for some reason that state seems to push the deception further than most. So why did Winters decide to join them rather than beat them? "A big reason for wanting to do this," he says, "is that I started here because I wanted to make single malt whiskey. I made what I thought was a great whiskey. It was a good whiskey. Once Dave Smith—I call him my assistant distiller; he's not an assistant distiller, he's a master distiller in his own right—once Dave took over selecting the barrels that went into each bottling, it became a great whiskey. Dave has a lot of patience, and he's got great blending skills. He took our single malt whiskey, which was a good product, and turned it great by blending."

Distilling is mostly science with a little bit of art around the edges. Blending, however, is mainly an art. It requires a well-tuned nose and palate, an acute sense memory, the ability to imagine flavors, and, of course, remarkable stamina. One of the people I most respect in the liquor business is John Glaser, a former marketing director at Johnnie Walker who started a company in 2000 called Compass Box that buys whiskies from around Scotland and blends them. His products are spectacular and very definitely crafted. Yet he distills nothing. It turns out that Glaser was also an inspiration for Breaking & Entering. "When we went out to do this we said, 'Think of this as an American whiskey Compass Box. John Glaser is one of the most talented people in the world."

Winters isn't content just to buy other people's bourbon, of course, even if he and Smith can make something great out of it. A few weeks before I visited St. George, a cereal cooker had been delivered. In order to ferment corn, you have to cook it first. As Winters explains: "When you're working with corn what you're trying to do is gelatinize the starches in it. You're breaking them open and making them available for conversion with the enzymes from the other malted grains. The way it's typically done is it's ground to the fineness of a polenta and then boiled with water. The other way is it goes through a heated roller mill and, as it's flattened under pressure and heat, the starch granules are exposed." There is another option, and of course Winters has explored it too. "Corn pops at 460 degrees, and then after it expands like that it cools down rapidly. I thought it'd be kind of fun to try that out because it also shifts the aromatics. I did do a small batch of popcorn bourbon." If he ever went into production with it, I'm sure it would be a big seller at the growing number of theaters that now offer cocktails to moviegoers.

But back to reality (always a challenge when dealing with Winters). St. George had already run some test batches of corn whiskey made from an Italian variety called red flint that was brought in from Italy by Bob Klein, co-owner of Oliveto Restaurant, in Oakland, and is now being grown organically near Davis, California. Combining that corn with conventionally grown rye and barley made a bourbon Winters liked, but something bigger was brewing in his mind. He'd found a farmer growing rye organically near Mt. Shasta and was planning on making an organic rye whiskey. "I started thinking we could use the organic rye," he explains, "and then I reached out to the guys at Sierra Nevada Brewing and said, 'I know you guys are growing your own barley, can we get some?' So we're going to be able to get enough barley from them to do a few small batches of a California, all-organic, three-farms bourbon."

Perhaps because his frame of reference is the single malt whiskey that brought him to distilling, Winters isn't particularly interested in casks. Single malts are generally aged in used barrels because barley spirit is more delicate than that made from corn or rye, and used barrels don't impart much flavor to the finished whiskey. There is a law that requires American single malt to be aged at least partially in new wood. (Presumably this was to protect American coopers, but as craft distillers become more influential, that might be another regulation to consider getting changed.) "I don't feel like whiskey is about the cooper's craft," Winters says. "It's about the distiller's craft. The cooper is the frame maker to my photography or my painting. It should accentuate it, it should make it really pop, but it shouldn't cover the whole thing. We use about 85 percent used bourbon barrels, 10 percent French oak, and 5 percent Port casks."

That said, Winters is hardly averse to experimenting with different barrel finishes. He has whiskey aging in old apple brandy casks; the thirtieth anniversary blend was finished in pear brandy barrels; there's some dry rye gin aging in used French and American wine casks ("just to see what it'll do); and he bought an empty barrel from a great California dessert-wine maker. "We've got an old Dolce barrel that we're experimenting with now. I feel like our whiskey tends to skew toward the sweeter side of things—even the new make is very sweet and chocolaty and malty—so I felt like that finish from the Dolce barrel might be really, really interesting."

What Winters is not likely to do is use small barrels, wood chips, or other shortcuts. Those who do, he feels, are making a fundamental mistake. "As they're looking to expedite the process," he says, "they're thinking that a greater surface area–to–volume ratio is the key. That gives you accelerated absorption of oak material, but you don't get the same oxidation, you don't get the same evaporative loss rate, which you want because you want to lose some of the higher alcohols. You don't want to get those overwhelming tannins from the American oak—at least I don't."

Given Winters's feelings about wood, it will be interesting to see the color of the local, organic bourbon when it's released. "We never color-correct our whiskies," he says, referring to the single malt. "Even some of our older stuff is fairly light in color, especially when you're looking at whiskey aged in an old bourbon barrel. Some of the French oak, because it's shaved and re-toasted, tends to go a little darker, but French oak seems to be lighter on the tannins anyway and gives more of the soft vanilla and cinnamon. I love what the barrels do for some things, but for me it's all about the distillation. That's where it all starts—barrel aging is more performance art."

Sometimes, however, an appreciative audience sees things that the "auteur" doesn't. When the audience is a bit of a genius in his own right, unexpected insight is not at all surprising. Thad Vogler, a co-owner of Bar Agricole, one of San Francisco's best cocktail destinations, was visiting St. George, and Winters decided to share one of the experiments. "Thad came over," says Winters. "We were smoking cigars and I pulled out the barrel-aged rum. I didn't have any plans to bottle it, but he said, 'You've got to bottle that. And I want it at cask strength.'"

Because the unaged version of that rum, which is called Agua Libre, is completely over-the-top, insanely aromatic, and grassier than any spirit I've ever tasted, I can understand why Winters might not have seen the commercial potential of the aged version. He did see my reaction to my first sip of Agua Libre, and he got a good laugh out of it. "I either want to blow your mind and make you love it or make you wonder why you set foot in here. It's got to be one or the other: I don't like beige emotions."

This is not a spirit you can be lukewarm about. If you like earth and funk, you'll love it. Unlike some rums that have off flavors as a result of problems during fermentation or fungus and bacteria infecting the cane that's been burned in preparation for harvesting, Agua Libre's funkiness is all from the plant. As Winters explains: "All the weirdness is a product of the cane itself. It's a funky mother. Our goal is to make sure there's a lot of there there." In that Winters succeeded, though he faced some daunting challenges along the way.

"I didn't like rum for the longest time," Winters says. "Too boring. The best of the rums had a lot of strong molasses qualities and that was okay, but it wasn't anything to scream about. Molasses is good as a flavoring agent in a dish, but there's nothing for me to love about molasses. Sugar cane, on the other hand, is good beyond the sweetness. It's got this beautiful grassy quality because sugar cane is, after all, a giant grass. So we started looking around for sugar cane growers in California. The first growers that we found were these Hmong farmers in Fresno who were growing it to celebrate Hmong New Year. This stuff is called Elephant Cane for a reason—it's hung like an elephant; it's massive, and we had to split each of these stalks in half with a machete to be able to get it to go through a mill. When it was all said and done it was a good rum, but it wasn't great. So we went back to the drawing board, and we tracked down another grower who was farther south, which made for a longer growing season, and he had smaller diameter sugar cane. Smaller diameter sugar cane is just like smaller grapes: more surface area, more flavor components. So as we crushed this stuff there was much more grassy aromas, and when we started distilling . . . it's grass, it's truffles, it's black olives, it's beautiful, earthy; it's got its own signature. So my problem was that rum wasn't funky enough. I might be a white guy, but I'm super funky."

Having found the right ingredient for the kind of rum he could get excited about, all that stood in the way of Winters completing the project was for him to survive the production process. After milling cane—twenty-five tons of cane—for five days to get enough juice to ferment and distill a batch, Winters came to work one morning ready to get down. "We were staging the cane juice in these 500-gallon tanks," he recalls. "They have a manhole cover on the top, and then in the center of that, there's a hole that you can put either an airlock on or just put a rubber bung in. We're getting ready to start pumping the stuff out of the tank, and I decide I'm going to take a look inside and see how it is. I climb up on a ladder and get over the tank—the bung's still in it so I figure there's no pressure in this thing. I undo the latch on the manhole and *boom!* The manhole hit the ceiling. It blew off like thirty feet. Inches from my face. It was an important safety lesson learned."

Things like that happen in part as a consequence of the improvisation that becomes necessary when you're trying new things. Most of the equipment at St. George is straight off the shelf. The stills, for example, are made by the venerable Holstein company, which claims to have outfitted more than five thousand distilleries worldwide. But for St. George to execute its vision it's sometimes necessary to improvise. Following on his account of near-decapitation, Winters begins a story clearly meant to top that one: "For years Jörg had wanted to make a Tequila here. We never had the wherewithal to do it until the vodka took off. Five years ago we had some extra cash, and Jörg reached out to people down in Mexico to find somebody who could supply us with agave. We found out that if we were going to ship agave across the border we were either going to have to fumigate it or cook it. Fumigation doesn't sound like a lot of fun to us, especially since there's always some sort of residue that's going to stick around that you don't want to distill over. The grower he found had a good relationship with a distiller in Tequila called Rubio, and at Rubio they agreed to throw the stuff into their autoclaves and cook it for us and then load it onto a refrigerated truck."

After a nerve-wracking five or six days of waiting while the US Department of Agriculture tried to figure out how to deal with the tank of *agave de miel*, which is basically the *jus* that runs off the agaves when they're cooked, and which Rubio had kindly included in the shipment, much to the confusion of the guys at the border, the cooked agave arrived at St. George.

Winters picks up the story: "We were told by a German engineer (and if you're going to trust anybody . . .) that the pump that we use for pumping all our fruit would be fine for pumping cooked agave. '*Ja, ja*, cooked agave, very soft, no problem.' We start throwing it in there, and the pump goes *woooorrrblllll* and stops. We break the pump. Well, okay, maybe if we cut it down. So we went out and bought a bunch of machetes and chainsaws to tear through this stuff. Machetes were slow; chainsaws we thought would be fast. They're not because they get gummed up with all the fiber. They cut through part of it, but they pull a bunch of fiber into the teeth, and then the whole thing looks like a great big stuffed-animal version of a chainsaw. Jörg suggested we throw it into the Mangler, which is a hammer mill we bought to crush quince. So we start throwing it in there, and it's going sort of okay until it starts throwing steel teeth out of the top. And the top is where you have to lean over to load it.

"So this is a Saturday. We've got to get through this stuff. We still have to get it into a tank because we want to do temperature-controlled fermentation. It's not working. I'm like, 'Okay, I'm going to outsmart this s--t.' I put in a call to a rental agency; I order a wood chipper. Wood chipper shows up. I'm like, 'Yeaaah, Who's your daddy now?' Within fifteen minutes of throwing this stuff into the wood chipper, the wood chipper's dead. It's clear we're not getting our deposit back.

"At that point I call Jörg; I say, 'It's not working; it was great to try, but I think we're f--ked.' He says, 'No, you're just not trying hard enough.' I'm like, 'Okay, what should I do?' He says, 'I don't know, think about it.' So I grabbed a bag of this stuff and went to a company in South San Francisco that sells industrial food-processing equipment. Somebody there has to have dealt with something like this at some point. I throw this bag on the guy's desk, and I say, 'What would you do if you wanted to get this ground up?' We go out into the yard, and he takes me to this industrial dog-food mill. He says, 'I can sell you this; I think it might work. It's used for taking frozen sides of beef and passing them through these little extrusion ports.'

"Get it back here, rewire the thing so it works with all our plugs and our current, and start throwing the stuff into it. Well, because the fibers are so long and so strong it's not extruding any of this through the plate, but it is softening the whole thing up. So at that point I run over to Rockwall Winery and get a whole bunch of half-ton fermentation bins. From the doors of the tasting room all the way out to the midsection of the distillery the floor was covered with these macro bins with softened agave; then we put water in there, and we put yeast in each one of these. The next day fermentation is going—the fiber's all in there because we're idiot eau de vie distillers, and that's what we have to do; it's very important to us to have all the solids present in the fermentation and the distillation—but because of the way this is all functioning, all the liquid's fermenting really strongly and lifting the solids, and the solids are all turning to vinegar. So we're trying to punch it down and realizing that punching it down is not working, and all it's going to do is get acetobacteria through the whole mass. So we stop doing that, and let it form a cap. Some solids are still taking part in the fermentation, and once the fermentation is done, we pull the top off of every one of those and discard probably half of our fermentable material and then start distilling the rest of it. There was still a lot of solids in there, so every time we opened up a drain on the still a trickle would come out, and then we'd have to get in with pitchforks and take the devil's furball, these boiling hot masses, out of the stills and then reload the still. We had burns all over our forearms; it was miserable.

"At the end of that, 40,000 pounds of agave piñas turned into 477 gallons of high-proof Tequila. That said, it's some of the best Tequila we've ever had. For a while it was going to be called 'Los Gringos Locos'—there are a number of things we called it—but ultimately you have to get TTB approval. My feeling was it didn't need to say Tequila, the important thing is the blue agave. You can say Tequila all day long, but if it doesn't say 100 percent blue agave, what's the point? And since we couldn't say Tequila on the label [because, like Champagne and Scotch, that name is a protected geographical indication], Agua Azul was born."

You'd think they'd have learned their lesson, but you wouldn't know these guys if you thought that. "This project is rearing its ugly head again," Winters says, a bit wearily. "Jörg is dissatisfied with retirement and wants to do something, and this is how it's manifesting. Right now we're under contract to buy a knife mill from a company in Mexico. Jörg wants to get a shipping container to turn into an oven and do a long, slow cook, like an oven-braise of agave, and we'll run it through the knife mill. If we're lucky, the knife mill will be able to get us sections of that fiber no longer than two inches. At that point . . . I'm not going to say."

The strange thing about all this is that people in Mexico have been successfully harvesting, cooking, fermenting, and distilling agaves for centuries. They didn't have machines that could extrude frozen sides of beef in Mexico hundreds of years ago. (Admittedly, the idea of St. George getting a mule and a giant millstone, digging a pit, and crushing the cooked agave that way may be a bit far-fetched, even for them.) What they do in Mexico today is run the cooked agave through a knife mill and then through a roller mill, the juices are extracted, and then fermented. Winters thinks that the key to Tequila's flavor is actually in what he calls the semisolids. "There's a gelatinous material that's wrapped into those fibers. My feeling is that all the character we're after is really in that. Jörg wants to have the other fibers in the process as well. There are a bunch of times when I've said, 'No, you're wrong; this is idiotic; we can't do this,' and too often he's proven me wrong, so we're going to give it a try and see what happens."

Disasters and near misses make the best stories, but I imagine flavored vodka looks like a pretty appealing alternative to the "devil's furball" when you're in the soup. St. George stopped making Hangar One for Proximo at the end of April 2014, so for the moment the simplest thing Winters makes is gin. Actually three gins, and actually they're not all that simple. The flagship is called Terroir, and the goal was to evoke the hillsides of northern California. It starts with grain neutral spirit and is redistilled with various botanicals in the Carter head in the still. Some gins are made by putting the botanicals in the body of the still, and Winters does do a bit of that; but most of the flavor extraction for his gins is accomplished in the vapors rather than the liquid. "Whenever I picture myself drinking a gin," he says, "I picture myself in a tuxedo, so the gin's got to be elegant—it's got to go with my outfit. We'd done some experiments where we ran the juniper berries in the pot, but the mechanical action of the boil actually starts pulling some elements that have a high boiling point over, and you get more acrid, more earthy qualities. However, if you put them in those baskets—it's called a Carter head, gin head, or botanicals basket—if you put them in there the vapor passes through them, and you have less of that entrainment so you have a more elegant expression of what the juniper berry is about. It's like smelling a juniper berry rather than chewing on one. We also put the bay leaves in there, and on our Botanivore Gin, we put fresh cilantro in there. If you put fresh cilantro in the pot it overcooks it, whereas up there it pulls the aromatics out and it doesn't give you those vegetal properties."

The most unusual flavor in the Terroir Gin comes from Douglas fir, but there's also bay laurel, coastal sage, fennel, wok-roasted coriander, cinnamon, orris root, and citrus peel in addition to the requisite juniper. It's very citrusy, which Winters says is in part a result of the bay laurel pushing the citrus elements forward. What I find most striking about all three St. George gins is the mouthfeel. My assumption was that the distillery might be using a particularly good grain neutral spirit, but Winters says that's not what I was experiencing. "It's the amount

of botanicals. The spirit we use for the gins, the job for that is to be a neutral canvas. It's the oils from all the botanicals that provide that richness, that roundness. We do a light filtration, some other people might do a heavier filtration, and they might do a little cold filtration, and that's going to strip a lot of those oils out as well."

Botanivore has an astounding nineteen different botanicals, most of which are steeped in the grain neutral spirit overnight. Despite the intensity of flavor, it still somehow maintains an elegance that I suspect will appeal to longtime gin drinkers. The third is barely a gin at all. Dry Rye is round, sweet, and somewhat peppery. All three are bottled at high proof—45 percent alcohol—with mixing in mind, and the Dry Rye combined with a good sweet vermouth and Campari makes a killer Negroni. If Winters ever gets the amaro he's been working on to the market, I want to be the first in line to try it and the Dry Rye in that classic cocktail.

There are very few craft distillers even playing with amari, and I've asked a lot of them about it. They're extremely popular in Italy, of course, and in this country in recent years one brand, Fernet Branca, has become what is often called a secret handshake for bartenders and patrons. Leopold Brothers, a Denver-based producer of excellent fruit liqueurs and some other interesting spirits, makes a Fernet that's quite good, but that's about it for Amari made in the United States. Winters has a theory about why amaro isn't a big seller here. "I think it's for the same reason that people were hard to get into things like absinthe: we don't like licorice, and we don't like

OPPOSITE: From left to right: Jörg Rupf, founder; Lance Winters, owner and master distiller; and Dave Smith, assistant distiller at St. George Spirits.

bitter. The reason that bitters work to stimulate your digestive process is because you're tricking your body into thinking it's poison. I loooove bitter. Our first stab at an amaro, we took grain alcohol and distilled that through rosemary and juniper and bay laurel. Into that we infused Seville orange peel, chinchona, wormwood, gentian, turkey rhubarb, white turmeric, cinnamon, lavender, orris root, and cola nut. I wanted to get something put together to figure out where I need to start shifting some of the flavors. I've got a pretty good idea. The process is half the fun. Making something you love is always a great moment because then you can share what was in your head with other people and they can get it. And when people get it, that's the greatest moment in the world."

RYE GIN OLD FASHIONED

Courtesy of Thad Vogler, Bar Agricole, San Francisco

1½ OZ. ST. GEORGE DRY RYE GIN
2 BAR SPOONS SMALL HAND FOODS GUM SYRUP
2 DASHES ORANGE BITTERS
2 DASHES AROMATIC BITTERS

☛ Combine all ingredients in a mixing glass filled with ice and stir. Serve in a rocks glass over a large cube of ice. Garnish with orange peel and a twist of lemon.

The country's largest producer of organic spirits is not in the Bay Area, near the foodie epicenters of San Francisco and Berkeley; it's not in the Pacific Northwest, with access to Seattle and Portlandia; and it's not in New York's Hudson Valley, a stonefruit's throw from Manhattan's magnificent greenmarkets. It's in downtown Los Angeles, practically in the shadow of the engineering marvel that is the I-5/I-10 interchange.

GREENBAR CRAFT DISTILLERY didn't start out to be an all-organic boozery, and it wasn't always in the concrete jungle. It began as Modern Spirits, in Monrovia, California, in the foothills of the San Gabriel Mountains, making a variety of infusions from conventional ingredients packaged in heavy, "perfume-quality" glass bottles. The combinations of ingredients Melkon Khosrovian and his wife, Litty Mathew, infused in purchased vodkas—potato and wheat—were not particularly conventional, and nearly a decade ago some seemed pretty radical: celery-peppercorn, pear-lavender, and black truffle, as well as the comparatively pedestrian candied ginger, chocolate-orange, grapefruit-honey, and tea.

The company was born out of Mathew's distaste for badly distilled vodka and the necessity of drinking it at the many Khosrovian family events the pair attended after getting engaged. Mathew is from southern India, and she's Cordon Bleu–trained. Watching her layer flavors as she cooked inspired Khosrovian to play with vodka in hopes of creating something they could toast with. He succeeded so well that before long cousins were calling and asking for three bottles for a party, then six bottles to take on vacation. But when a stranger called asking for some, they decided it was time to change their phone number or think about doing it as a career.

From the beginning, their intention was to open in Los Angeles, but when they went to the planning department to find out where a distillery would be allowed, they were told to look up the appropriate rules in the massive codebook. Sensing the beginning of a Kafkaesque ordeal, they expanded their search. When they approached officials in Monrovia they were met with open arms, so that's where they launched their business.

The infusion recipes were the result of extensive experimentation, and the switch to organics was a consequence of noticeable changes in flavor over time. The recipes had remained the same, but the balance they'd worked so hard to achieve was gone. The flavors had become more assertive. Conversations with the farmers supplying their fresh produce led to the

discovery that, in every case, they had recently transitioned to organic farming. Further investigation moved the couple to shift all their production to organic ingredients, and that in turn led to efforts to minimize the company's carbon footprint, starting with a switch to lighter bottles and labels made from 100 percent post-consumer waste.

In 2011, when their building in Monrovia was slated for demolition to make way for an extension of a light rail line, they found they were no longer being ignored by the city of Los Angeles; they were in fact being courted. The city was trying to attract "green" businesses to underutilized industrial buildings near the Los Angeles River, and the mayor's office saw the potential in a sustainability-minded distiller. Loans were available through LA's Community Redevelopment Agency, and after buying its building, Greenbar secured one for $250,000 that allowed the company to buy additional equipment.

One thing Greenbar didn't buy was a machine to zest the two thousand pounds of lemons necessary for a batch of its Tru lemon vodka. The lemons are hand-zested to avoid any of the bitter, white pith making its way into the infusion. The crew also splits and scrapes vanilla beans for their Tru vanilla vodka. (Make of this what you will: Mathew says half the crew is allergic to lemon; the other half is allergic to vanilla.) "We use two kinds of vanilla," says Mathew. "We use Madagascar for the body and the depth of flavor, and we use Tahitian, which is not even a vanilla bean, for the aroma." Because it's not sweet—there's no sugar added—it plays well with food. Mathew has a favorite cocktail to have with dinner. "We eat a certain amount of Indian food at home. I love our vanilla vodka

OPPOSITE: Melkon Khosrovian and Litty Mathew of Greenbar Craft Distillery, Los Angeles, California.

with lime juice, curry leaves, and some simple syrup. I shake it hard with ice, and when it's finished I sprinkle some powdered toasted-cumin seed on top."

Greenbar's liqueurs, under the Fruitlab label, are unusual in that the base is rum rather than the usual neutral grain spirit. Because rum is made from sugar (cane and/or molasses), the increased perception of sweetness means less sugar is needed in the liqueur. The rum flavor is noticeable if you're sipping the liqueurs, but less so in a cocktail, which is generally how they are used. After playing around with the orange liqueur, I found that my recipes had to be adjusted slightly. For example, a Margarita needed a little more liqueur than usual (I like my sours sour), and the flavor that lingered longest was orange. This may be a testament to their revelation that organic produce is more intensely flavored and aromatic, which they attribute to the plants' need to protect themselves using their only defenses: flavor and aroma.

"Unusual" might be the word I most associate with Greenbar spirits, and not just because so many of their flavors are uncommon in the spirits world. The rum makes use of a controversial winemaking technique: micro-oxygenation. Like much of what the distiller does, this experiment was an attempt to address a shortcoming. "One of the big issues I have with white rum," says Mathew, "is that you can't taste that it's a rum spirit. I want to know that I'm having a rum drink, even after putting all the fresh ingredients on top of it. White rum is put into barrels, and then it's charcoal filtered. I understand the mellowing in barrel, but charcoal filtering takes out all this flavor. So I kept saying to Melkon, 'This doesn't make sense.' I understand that white rum is functional, and I understand why Bacardi wanted to make a white rum—they wanted something to compete with vodka—but why can't it taste like rum?

We were aware that micro-oxygenation was used to soften red wines so we decided to see if it would work on rum. Over the course of three or four days we did notice a difference. We were able to mellow out the white rum using micro-oxygenation; we didn't have to age it in wood, and we didn't have to filter it. It helps us keep the flavors we want."

PUMP IT UP

Greenbar was not the only producer I saw using a version of micro-oxygenation as part of its barrel-aging process. Downslope, in Englewood, Colorado, uses pumps from aquariums to bubble air through some of its whiskey barrels for eight hours per week. The idea is an intriguing one, given that the smaller barrels being used by so many craft whiskey makers contribute lots of wood flavor without providing much of the oxidation that only comes over time. Cleveland Whiskey says its Black Reserve Bourbon is "finished with an oxygen-enriched, accelerated aging process." Unfortunately, the aging process is much more complex than simply adding wood and oxygen (or even "rapid pressure changes," as Cleveland also says it does), and so far no shortcut seems to be as effective as time and well-made barrels of a certain volume.

Another thing Greenbar does that's very unusual for an American craft distillery is make Tequila. It's called Ixá, and of course it can't be made in Los Angeles and be called Tequila, so Greenbar takes a little bit of Los Angeles to Mexico. After much scouting around, Khosrovian found a company that would let him take over its distillery for a few days at a time and make an agave spirit in a way that remains consistent with his point of view. Instead of using an autoclave—essentially a large pressure cooker—the agaves are roasted for three days in clay ovens. After the roasted agave is crushed, the liquid is fermented in the presence of the agave fibers, the way St. George Spirits likes to do it, to maximize flavor. These are not the modern, industrial techniques, but Ixá is a very bright, aromatic spirit with a bit of appealing vegetal funk.

Until the spring of 2013, Mathew and Khosrovian's vodkas were made using purchased neutral grain spirit. The usual question arises: Is that craft? I think the flavored vodkas fit that description. There's great care taken in sourcing the ingredients, they developed the techniques used to achieve the flavors they wanted, and the end results are delicious. Very few small distillers make their own neutral grain spirit; there are plenty of good commercial ones available. And making something "neutral" is the opposite of what most craft distillers are trying to do. Mathew also makes the point that for a straight vodka to actually be neutral it "has to go through that kind of column distillation," which is an industrial process. Just a few months after that conversation with Mathew, Greenbar bought a small-scale, continuous fractionating column still so that it could begin producing its own neutral grain spirit. The

OPPOSITE: When Greenbar's suppliers started to farm organically, Melkon Khosrovian noticed that the flavors and aromas were more intense.

still has what Mathew calls "virtual plate capability—meaning it can make low-proof to neutral-proof spirits by letting us dial in an exact output proof with very precise heads and tails separations." And, she adds, "we can run it at 20 percent of the power of our pot still, so making flavorful spirits will be much more economical than on our pot still." There are potential long-term cost savings, and Greenbar will have greater control of the product, not to mention insurance against the rising price of the already expensive organic neutral grain spirit (it runs two to four times the price of conventional NGS), but even for a craft distiller, this level of commitment is unusual. It is, however, a logical step for a company as uncompromising and committed to craft and sustainability as Greenbar is.

In 2007 Mo Heck, her husband, Al, and their friend Mac Kenney II built a still out of an empty beer keg. For two and a half years the three amigos played with that starter still until it got, as Mo says, "a little out of hand." Through trial and error and Mo's obsessive study, their vodka had gotten a little too good, and they were starting to attract a bit too much attention. "Our booze would show up to parties before we would," she says. "People would be like, 'Oh, I love your booze; who are you?' We either had to shut it down or get legal. So we've been legal since November 13, 2010, but it took us eight months to get our certificate of occupancy from the city—in their defense, they thought we would blow up the town with our stills."

Mo moved from kegs to kettles, buying industrial steam kettles on eBay, and designed a series of increasingly complex distilling apparatuses that, with the help of her neighbor Joe who's a plumber (but not *that* Joe the Plumber), now fill the rear section of **PROJECT V DISTILLERY & SAUSAGE COMPANY**, in Woodinville, Washington, with copper tubing, vents, and gauges. "Each of the stills started as drawings on bar napkins," says Mo. "We bring them to Joe, and we build them together. Without him we wouldn't be where we are today. If anything goes wrong in there, we can get him to fix it."

The raw material for everything Project V makes is white winter wheat from Mo's aunt and uncle's farm, in eastern Washington. "It's really high in starch and low in protein," says Mo. "It's perfect for ramen noodles. Or vodka." The wheat is milled on site. (In the early days, milling was done on a small hand mill inside Stella, a gutted VW bus, to keep the dust down; it

would take Mo six hours to crank out a batch of wheat.) Then it's fermented in big plastic barrels and distilled in the ever-growing collection of stills. Project V makes five vodkas: an 80-proof filtered lightly with charcoal, a more-heavily filtered 80 proof, an unfiltered 100 proof, a chai-infused 80 proof, and (believe it or not) a 160 proof that bartenders love to use for bitters, tinctures, and flaming drinks. (Please do not try that at home.)

Vodka doesn't get much attention in the craft spirits world, and for good reason: most of it (even ones with words like "handcrafted" on the label) is industrially made. But Project V (the V is for vodka, by the way) makes tiny batches—just five gallons at a time. The heads and tails cuts are severe, which is why all its spirits have a rich mouthfeel, and why the 160-proof bottling is actually palatable. Another thing Mo insists on is that the vodka be distilled to 190 proof. (Everything is diluted from there to bottling proof.) The legal definition of vodka in the United States includes the requirement that it reach 190 proof, but as Al explains, that's not so easy and not always complied with: "We have to do another entire thirty-hour run to get from 188 to 190. So a lot of people who make vodka stop at 188 then filter it, filter it, filter it. But if you do that, you didn't truly make what the Feds define as vodka. There are a lot of ways to skirt the system, but Mo will not. Mo runs the show here, and everything is—from grain to bottle—100 percent the real deal."

Demand for Project V's vodka is high, and the process is slow, so it can be a struggle to keep up. That's a good problem to have and a much better problem than some others

OPPOSITE: The bases of the stills at Project V Distillery, in Woodinville, Washington, are steam kettles bought on eBay.

ABOVE: Mo Heck, distiller, at work at the Project V Distillery.

the distiller has had. In 2012, Washington State began the transition from state-controlled liquor stores to the more common privately owned system in place in all but eighteen states. That nearly put Project V out of business. "Under the state system," Mo says, "there were 326 liquor stores. To get listed, they give you an appointment, and you have fifteen minutes to tell your story; they taste your product; and if you can support 326 liquor stores, they'll list you. We were on the special-order list—which means if you try our vodka here and you like it, you can go to your liquor store and ask for it, and they'll get it—but we weren't listed yet. We were working on building more stills so we could support 326 stores. We had an appointment December 8. But on November 6, Proposition

1183 passed; they cancelled all appointments and stopped buying from us. By February we were sunk. We couldn't pay our
rent. Al saved us. He gave us enough money to pay our rent
and buy our ingredients for long enough that we could get
through December and sign with a distributor. So here we are,
nine months later not able to keep up with demand."

As with so much of what it does, Project V inverts the
usual craft-spirits model: rather than make vodka for cash flow
while waiting for the whiskey to age, it's fully committed to
vodka. Mo and Al have made a tiny amount of whiskey—also
wheat, of course—and it's aging in big barrels. Because they
can't keep up with the vodka demand, however, it's unlikely
ever to become a major part of their production. After a great
deal of experimentation they finally settled on a gin recipe
they were happy with: their 80-proof vodka infused with
juniper, rose petals, orange peel, honey, and almonds. And
then there's the sausage part of the company name. The spent
grain left over after fermentation goes to Bucking Boar Farm,
in Snohomish, Washington, and comes back in the form of
pork (some of which it turns into sausage) that is sold at the
distillery. It's the great, big, beautiful wheat-booze-bacon
circle of life.

The still at Osocalis.

CHAPTER 7

CALIFORNIA IS FOR BRANDY LOVERS

Two of America's oldest—and best—craft distillers are in California. This seems perfectly appropriate given that the only state more associated with mood-altering substances is the state of inebriation. That both **GERMAIN-ROBIN** and Osocalis built their reputation on brandy also makes sense: the Golden State grows some mighty fine grapes. Another thing both houses share is a tremendous debt to a Frenchman named Hubert Germain-Robin, and also to that nearly extinct West Coast tradition, hitchhiking.

Hubert Germain-Robin is from a very long line of Cognac producers: Jules Robin & Co. was established in 1782 and remained in the family until it was sold to Martell in 1964. When a former Berkeley classics professor named Ansley Coale stopped to pick up Hubert and his wife, Carole, on a remote stretch of Highway 101 in 1981, it wasn't just his family history that made the thirty-year-old Frenchman seem weary. By the time the couple reached California they'd already traveled from Quebec to British Columbia and were working their way down the Pacific Coast, with South America their ultimate destination. Coale offered the couple a place to stay, and, in the course of their visit, Hubert told the story of how the traditional distillation methods of Cognac were being abandoned in favor of more efficient industrial techniques. A plan was hatched to make brandy on Coale's Mendocino County ranch, and within a year Hubert had acquired a traditional still from Cognac and

OPPOSITE: In the early eighties Hubert Germain-Robin imported traditional equipment from Cognac to make brandy in California.

shipped it to northern California. By 1983 he'd begun to apply those old-time distillation methods to New World grapes.

Even in wine country, however, which grapes to use was a question. "The perceived wisdom in Cognac is that the grapes don't matter," says Coale. "Where they get their quality is from limestone in the soil—Grand Champagne has a ton of limestone, Petite Champagne has less limestone—so their feeling is that it doesn't matter what grapes you use. Here we are, in America, and Hubert's saying to me, 'Let's use Thompson seedless out of Fresno for eighty dollars a ton.' I was thinking of the logistics: we're going to be driving down to Fresno to tell guys how to make the wine; if there's a problem, we're driving down to Fresno again. So I started talking to some of the local wineries, and at that time you could buy grapes from somewhere between $225 and $400 a ton. This is 1982, 1983. Some huge proportion of the grapes grown here were being sold to Gallo

to flavor their jug wines. They didn't care if it was red or white. So we were able to find fabulous grapes. Somebody sold us some Pinot Noir; we picked early because Hubert's frame of reference was Cognac: fifteen brix! Gotta pick 'em! [Brix is a measure of sugar, and therefore ripeness, in fruit; wine grapes tend to be harvested in the low to mid-twenties.] He was worried about losing acid. The grower said, 'These things are like bullets, you don't want 'em.' Hubert said, 'Yes, we do; this is how we do it.' The learning curve was pretty steep. He wanted Vaslin presses—crushers instead of more modern bladder presses—he wanted to ferment in open-air tanks because that's how they do it in Cognac. There was foam all over the place. The first year we only ran about twenty barrels, just to find out, to learn all this stuff. And we never bought grapes out of Fresno."

Although Hubert Germain-Robin is no longer involved with the company (he now has a distillation consulting business and wrote a book called *Traditional Distillation Art & Passion*), Coale continues to express his tremendous respect for Hubert's accomplishments. "The guy's a great distiller," says Coale, "but he had to teach himself how to do the work in the cellar. We bought some Sémillon in 1987, and we made five barrels of it. Four years later Hubert said, 'There's nothing here.' We started blending some of it into what we were calling Fine Alambic Brandy. In 1994, the Sémillon exploded. It was fabulous. The only way we had to find out was to make it and sit on it for seven f--king years! To be making the products he made from scratch, with no reference whatsoever. . . ." Even nearly twenty years later, Coale has a hard time finding the words to express his amazement.

The brandies, now made at an old Fetzer Vineyards facility, near Ukiah, are delicious. They have earned worldwide critical acclaim and have been served at the White House. But thirty years after firing up that first still, the company's success is also its greatest challenge. "The most pressing thing we have going right now," says Coale, "is figuring out how can we sell fifteen hundred cases a year of something that's more than fifteen years old. When we've got that done, we've made it."

The main weakness I see in recent arrivals to craft distilling is that the vast majority of their aged spirits are being released too young or with shortcuts taken. So it's not just a little ironic that one of the few companies that actually has a commercial quantity of well-aged brown spirits ready to be released would have a hard time selling them. Brandy isn't the easiest thing to market, of course, which seems doubly perplexing given how far wine culture has come in the United States. Though there was a time when only French wine was taken seriously, there's clearly no resistance to premium California wine: Cabernet Sauvignon from Napa Valley routinely fetches prices north of $100 a bottle. When you consider that it takes roughly 1,600 gallons of wine to make 250 gallons of 40 percent alcohol spirit, and that 2 to 4 percent of the spirit is lost annually to evaporation, a bottle of Germain-Robin XO, made up of brandies that are generally at least seventeen years old, starts to seem like a bargain at $120. And that's just the beginning. Germain-Robin buys three or four different Pinot Noirs every year. "We keep the varietals, or even individual vineyards, segregated," Coale explains. "We vinify them, distill them, and age them separately because that gives us the maximum complexity when we blend. Something we're going to sell in seven years we'll begin to put together after two or three years. But the older stuff, the stuff that'll go into the XO, it'll be twelve or thirteen years before we start doing the blend. Another thing we do, we dilute with rainwater.

That's important. Distilled water's flat and dead; rainwater's alive and beautiful. We tend to cut it a little bit at the beginning because the slower you cut it down to bottling proof the better. We like to do it 4 or 5 percent at a time. It takes somewhere around nine months to recover from [each dilution]. We'll start that reduction process practically right away, especially something we're going to use in six or seven years. The XO we might put away at distillation proof. Then the real work begins."

That may sound like an absurd overstatement given the amount of work that's been done to that point, but there are fourteen hundred barrels in the cellar—representing some fifty-seven thousand cases of finished brandy—each of which has to be tasted periodically. As Coale points out, "The hidden part of our business is that 85 percent of it is in the cellar. We show the still, and everybody goes, 'Oh wow, the still!' But you have to know what's inside every one of the barrels, and that's a huge job." It's also a costly one—the vast majority of the company's assets are sequestered in wood casks, each of which costs around a thousand dollars, so it's not surprising that it took nearly fifteen years for the company to see a positive cash flow. And that, in large part, was the impetus for developing a vodka brand, Hangar One, and why Coale continues to look for opportunities to create new brands.

Hangar One started in 2001 as a joint venture with the great eau-de-vie producer St. George Spirits (see Chapter 6), with Coale leading the marketing and St. George overseeing

OPPOSITE: Ansley J. Coale, cofounder of Germain-Robin.

production. They shared the goal of continuing to make and sell the products at the heart of their respective companies, brandy and eaux de vie. Each took out a $500,000 line of credit—which quickly proved inadequate—but by 2006 sales were $8.5 million. In 2010, Coale sold his stake in the brand to the spirits conglomerate Proximo, which owns Jose Cuervo and more recently bought Stranahan's Colorado Whiskey (see Chapter 9). The return on that investment has allowed Coale to move forward on projects with slightly shorter waiting periods for revenue than brandy. "We gave ourselves a mandate," says Coale. "To take our share of the Hangar One money—it was 80 percent of our revenues—and try to recover those revenues by doing other things. I'm trying to raise money for the whiskey project now. We think we can do ten thousand cases a year. That requires a cellar of forty-five thousand cases. Your negative cash flow during that period is going to be somewhere between three-and-a-half and four million dollars. You can lay off a little of that by selling a bit along the way, but that's a ten-year project."

As much as lovers of craft spirits hate it when a favorite brand is sold, success is only going to attract more attention to the Hangar Ones, Stranahan's, and Tuthilltowns of the world. And ultimately, with a bit of patience, these acquisitions may be good for their fans. The money St. George and Germain-Robin earned from the sale of Hangar One is being put to good use: both companies are working on new products that likely would not have been possible without Proximo's money. Economic reality also points to another cold truth: craft distillers can't afford to get too emotionally attached to their product. Coale recalls that "when the buyer showed up, they wanted the brand. I'm not sure that if you're not willing to sell at a certain point whether you can justify a three-and-a-half to four million dollar investment over a ten-year period. If somebody puts up the three-and-a-half to four million dollars, he'll be able to push a button that says Sell Me. And then we can do something else."

One of the something elses Coale is doing now is, believe it or not, a line of bottled cocktails called Fluid Dynamics. In May 2011 Coale was out talking to various bartenders in San Francisco. "We were trying to get them to do with our brandy what they're doing with good bourbons. So one guy says, 'I'm going to mix some of this up and put it in a small barrel.' And the next place I go, the guy there says the same thing! So I go, 'We can do that.' Four months later, after making some experimental blends with our Craft Method Brandy and Andy Quady's VYA sweet vermouth, putting them in the small barrels, and tasting them two weeks later so we'd have some idea of what was really going to happen—turns out you can't use bitters, and if you use the standard proportion of vermouth, it takes over—four months later we had product on the market, and it's already 15 percent of our sales. I'm really proud of it. A big company couldn't do this. They wouldn't let their production people do it. They'd have somebody sitting there saying, 'Oh, this should be sweeter because that's what the consumer likes, let's put some sugar in it.'"

Another ongoing project is Low Gap whiskey. Because of licensing regulations the company has had to create a business arrangement with one of its distillers, Crispin Cain, who works on his grain spirits in a separate area of the distillery. Coale says, "Our notion is that it's easier to sell four different twenty-five-hundred-case whiskies than it is to sell ten thousand of one. In 2010–11 we made wheat; this year [2012] we developed a corn. We recently made our first batch of rye, and we're trying to figure out whether we want to do oat or barley for the fourth one. See, we're Cognac distillers, so we're not thinking about the mash so much: make really good corn mash, distill it, and then if you think it needs some rye, don't worry about the mash. You've got rye there that has its own complexities, separate, that you can blend in. There'll be wheat, corn, rye, and whatever else, but they might contain some admix of the others as we go. Our sense is you get a little more complexity when you do it that way." Most of the whiskey is in wood, but a small amount of the wheat, the corn, and the rye have been released as individual white whiskies. All are produced on one of the two antique alambic (that's the French spelling of alembic) stills that Germain-Robin bought from the company whose Cognacs it imports, Maison Surrenne.

Cain has also recently released three gins under the Russell Henry label: a London Dry style, one made with the leaves and fruit of a lime native to Malaysia called *limaupurut*, and another that is infused and distilled with Hawaiian white ginger. A gin aged for a year in oak is scheduled for an October 2014 release. There are also a few liqueurs in the portfolio, and a sister company imports some excellent mezcals (Los Danzantes, Los Nahuales, Mezcalero, and Alipus). The company's noncompete agreement with Proximo expired in April 2013, so Coale and Cain, along with Cain's son, Devin, were able to develop a line of flavored vodkas.

To say the least, there's a lot going on, but if Coale has learned anything in twenty years of selling high-end California brandy and luxury fruit-flavored vodkas it's how to sell craft spirits. He does so in a way, he says, "that presents them for what they really are and doesn't ask them to be something they aren't. The only thing that works is to have people who interface with the consumer—bartenders, store clerks—who believe in your product enough to talk about it. We've sold a couple million bottles by having bartenders say, 'This stuff is made by a couple of guys in California, and it's really good because they use real ingredients and they really care about what they're doing.' You can't do anything else. Anything else you do makes you look like something you're not."

OSOCALIS has a lot in common with Germain-Robin. It's situated in a great wine-growing area and takes full advantage of that fact, its brandy-making equipment and techniques are extremely traditional, and the two distilleries are only about two hundred miles apart. But the differences are even more striking. You won't see a gin, vodka, or bottled cocktail wending its way down the twisty mountain roads between San Jose and Santa Cruz. You won't hear much talk of branding and probably even less about positive cash flow. When owner Dan Farber, who is also an old friend and longtime admirer of Hubert Germain-Robin, lets slip that Osocalis was founded in the early 1990s to make apple brandy, it becomes even more obvious that making money was not the primary motivation for getting into the spirits game.

In his best faux-French accent, Farber recounts a discussion he had with Hubert at the time. "He said to me, 'You are going to produce only apple brandy? Uhhh, the market for great brandy in the United States is a million cases per year. It is very difficult for us to achieve even a very small market share. Apple brandy—ees impossible.' I was like, 'Oooooooh, maybe I should change my business plan.' Which we did, but also because apple brandy takes so much longer than grape brandy. Apple brandy starts as a much hotter, fierier spirit, and it takes a lot longer to supple it up—for me it's really twenty-five-plus years."

Hubert wasn't the only one who questioned Farber's business plan. Randall Grahm, the brilliant and iconoclastic winemaker who had also set up shop in the Santa Cruz Mountains, put it bluntly, as Farber recalls. "Randall said to me, 'Distillery? You are f--king crazy. Nobody can do that.' I said, 'What about Germain-Robin?' He said, 'Ansley is a marketing genius.'" (Left unsaid, presumably, was that Farber did not appear to be a marketing genius.)

As if a distillery wasn't enough of a stretch at the time, Farber's other revenue stream, while he waited for the apple brandy to come around, was cider. "We were producing a traditional,

Pyrenees-style dry cider—not sparkling, totally naturally fermented, dry. I thought cider was going to be the next big thing. Within three years I dropped it. The problem, even now, is that the part of the market that should be interested in it—the wine drinkers—is the part of the market that is not interested in it, and you're not going to get them interested in it. I thought wine drinkers would migrate over to a really well-made cider because it's a natural in the summertime or with a lunch where you don't want high alcohol but you want that fruit and a little bit of acidity and tannin. But, anyway, that didn't happen. And the beer drinker's already got beer."

Having dropped cider and put the apple brandy on a very low and slow back burner, Farber turned to distilling local wine grapes. "The art is to try to get the essence of great fruit, wherever it comes from," he says. "We don't drink grape juice with dinner; we drink wine because of that transformative character that fermentation gives to that grape juice. In the same way, we ferment the fruit and then extract from it the entire essence of the fermented wine. Then we put it in barrels for long periods of time to again have it undergo a transformative process and produce something new."

Farber studied distillation in France, and he and his partner, Jeff Emery, the proprietor and winemaker at Santa Cruz Mountain Vineyards, apply traditional French methodology to New World wines. "Our vinification techniques are different; our wines are slightly different. We're looking for the same quality characteristics, but they're expressed differently in California wine, so our distillation and aging techniques are perturbed slightly from the absolutely classic house styles. But everything

OPPOSITE: Osocalis, in northern California, uses a 100-gallon antique Charentais still.

we do, except for the use of these different grape varieties, would be legal in Cognac or calvados."

The best California wines have the rich, ripe fruit that you'd expect from grapes grown there, but that relentless sunshine also imposes certain demands—controlling yields and making smart picking decisions to avoid losing acidity and ending up with an alcohol bomb, to name two—in order to achieve the balance that makes a truly great wine. Making great brandy in California presents similar opportunities, and equal challenges.

"It would've been a lot cheaper," says Farber, "for me to fly over to Cognac every year, visit with my friends, bring back two cases, pay the duty, have a nice trip to France, and drink Cognac for the rest of my life than to do this! I didn't really need to make brandy unless I felt there was something we could do here that was truly world class. It may not be in my lifetime; I may just be setting the path. I thought that what Hubert was doing at that time in Ukiah had those characteristics. There was something truly great that was being done there. I mean, Hubert would give me brandy. We're good friends. I didn't need to produce my own just to drink brandy."

Even with his access to Hubert and his own training in Cognac, the greatness that Farber was looking for required a lot of trial and error. "I'm a bit of a traditionalist," the native New Yorker says. "Yet I do understand the need to move things forward in a smart way. And that takes experimentation. But it takes a deep understanding of how and why we've gotten to the place we're at now. Why is Scotch the way it is now? Why is bourbon the way it is now? Why is Cognac the way it is now? It wasn't because there was a bunch of idiots for the past three

OPPOSITE: Dan Farber, co-owner and founder of Osocalis.

hundred years that didn't know what the f--k they were doing. There were very, very bright people who thought a lot about this, who had great palates, who got us to the point we're at now. That doesn't mean that there's no room for innovation, but you have to have an extremely healthy respect for how and why we're at the point we're at now. You have to first understand how we got here before you can move forward. And you also, believe it or not, have to have a deep understanding of the nature of experimentation. Experimentation is 99.999999999 percent failure! So if you do something new, you should expect it to be bad, or at least less good than what came before. It happens in plant breeding; it happens in everything we do. Evolution is mostly failed branches. We got to where we are here because of God knows how many species, how many mutations—that gene mutated, you die! So most experiments fail. And yet, the ones that don't fail are the ones that produce new and novel and interesting things. You have to experiment, but you have to

continuously experiment and not expect your first experiment to be a thing that nobody knew about for three hundred years."

It's impossible not to notice the veiled criticism of some of his fellow craft distillers. And it doesn't take long for Farber to make that criticism explicit. "The notion is," he says of unnamed newcomers, "the business plan says that 'no matter what, I'm drawing a good salary in two years. So whatever we produce in year two has to be great. Especially in brown spirits.' Is that a reasonable expectation? Not really."

The Osocalis business plan obviously did not project that whatever was produced in year two would be great. In fact, it took thirteen years for Osocalis to offer its brandy for sale. Let that sink in for a moment. "I said, 'I won't release a bottle until I think it would be more interesting to drink ours,'" says Farber. "It took a long time for me not to say, 'You know what? I'd rather grab that bottle of Germain-Robin or that bottle of Cognac or that Armagnac or that calvados, and let's just let ours stay there.' But there was this point, at thirteen years, where Hubert said, 'You need to be in the market. I am going to come down, we are going to blend, you are going to bottle.' So we did."

Why did it take so long? Without restrictive laws like those governing the production of Cognac, wouldn't it be possible—even likely—that a brandy made from better grapes and aged in different wood could be delicious sooner? Farber tried every possible combination in search of the right cask. He says he wasn't looking for that oxymoronic holy grail of small distillers everywhere, "faster" aging, but rather the right flavors for his brandies. "We had wood that was sourced from three forests, aged in the Southeast, coopered in California; we had the same forests aged in California, coopered in California; we took American oak from other sources, aged it in France, coopered it in France. No matter what we did, American oak wants to make that bourbon character, and it just doesn't really go well with fruit. We use 100 percent French oak because, after twenty years of experimentation, we found that the tannin structure of French oak supported fruit much better than American oak. I didn't really want to import wood from Europe—each one of these barrels costs us fifteen hundred bucks instead of three or four hundred—I would've rather sourced it in the United States. American oak does go well with many grain-based distilled spirits. But for fruit it just didn't work."

French oak is tighter-grained than American oak, and therefore less permeable, so the effect of the wood on the spirit is diminished. There are specific qualities that are present only in spirits that spend long periods of time in cask, most famously *rancio*, which is said to begin to develop around ten years of age, with the first aromas being floral. It continues to metamorphose, moving into spicy notes and later tropical fruit, with flavors most often described as nutty and mushroomy. It's a phenomenon most often associated with Cognac, but *rancio* can sometimes be found in very old Scotch whisky as well. Farber believes that the key to developing this element is a "whole set of microflora and microfauna that grows on the barrel and in the *chai*." (The chai is the warehouse where brandies are stored in cask, and much is made of the different styles of Cognac that come from aging in a "dry" chai as opposed to a "wet" chai.)

"Part of the aging process of great brown spirits is the aging of the warehouse," Farber continues. "You don't get as much of that in bourbon because you have this rotation of new barrels in. You get a little bit of it in the rickhouse itself, but it never really gets to permeate the wood or penetrate into the whiskies because you never have that rich development of microflora on the barrels. Here, from the inception, we knew we needed to age the building, the barrels, the whole thing. You'll never get that kind of character by just throwing spirit in a cask and putting it in a metal building. It's not to say it's necessarily bad or good, but if you like it that's the only way to get it."

That, of course, raises the question of what Farber is looking for, though there's no question what he isn't looking for. Throughout our conversation he would often use American whiskey as a point of comparison, probably in deference to my greater familiarity with bourbon than Cognac. The irony is that he readily admits he doesn't really like bourbon. "But I get the quality factors," he says. "And I think that if I was with a bunch of bourbon drinkers, we would all agree on which the good ones were and which the bad ones were. I've had a few where I've thought, that really did get the damn oak integrated. It's quite an achievement. Every time I visit those places, I'm so impressed with how much knowledge they have of how the grain and the oak are going to interact. Elijah Craig Twelve Year Old? For twenty-five bucks! Holy s--t! I can't do that. Only they can. Heaven Hill? Those boys, they know what the f--k they're doing. Where I think bourbon typically falls short is that you're usually left with two components: the beautiful grain spirit and the oak. And they never come together in one piece. The same thing happens when you put young oak on a young brandy: you have fruit and oak, and it takes time for those things to marry. And in fact, if you put too much oak on, you'll never get them to marry. That's why we only put a small percentage of new oak on the brandies. The remainder has to be neutral oak, so we have to import neutral oak casks.

"What you want is the marriage of the fruit and the wood to produce new things that come through the aging process. So notes of dried fruits and nuts and a little bit of citrus peel—dried orange peel—a little of the leathery, cedary character. None of those are present in the young eau de vie. And none of them come directly from the wood. They come through development in barrel of wood and spirit. It's not just, 'Ooh, that's smooth!' That's easy. That's the trivial thing. If you can't have something that doesn't hurt you . . . that's sort of entry-level stuff. The real art is to produce flavors that, just like wine, still have the flavor of the grape yet have all these new things that make it so interesting. Great brown spirits should do the same thing: they should have the flavor of the beast that they came from and produce new things that are not present in the wine. Complexity is the number one goal for great brandy and for great brown spirits of all kinds. Whiskey tends to favor slightly more intense flavors, brandies somewhat less intense, but we look for what the French call *finesse*, which really translates to length. The wood, the aging, the surface area–to–volume ratio, where in the chai the brandy is aging . . . these are some of the things that determine the ability to get *finesse*. And these are characteristics that have been known to the French for centuries."

In France, brandies are aged for decades. As Farber points out, "Brandy is the only brown spirit that can beneficially spend time in wood for the time scale of a human life. If I taste a Grand Champagne that's younger than forty-five years old, I say, 'Why am I even bothering?' I should be drinking a Bons Bois or a Borderie or a Fins Bois [these are three of the six regions, or *crus*, of Cognac, along with Grand Champagne and Petite Champagne at the high end and Bois

Ordinaire at the low end] that would be at its peak maturity at twenty-five or thirty-five years. They're just gorgeous. The Grand Champagne is still tight at twenty-five. At thirty-five it's still kind of like, "Huh?' At forty-five you start to see, 'Ooooh!' And then at sixty-five, it's like, 'OOOOOOHHH!' And if you taste really great ones at eighty-five or a hundred years old, it's like, 'I get it now.' But that's eighty-five or a hundred years. The great Grand Champagnes are just amazing. The Louis XIII chais, the whole building, have been aging for centuries. The barrels are from the 1700s!

"In California we don't know what we have here, really. I'm cautiously optimistic because Hubert's best brandies, now at thirty-five-plus years, are still improving. But it'll take another generation or two. Will our brandies go for sixty or eighty years? Don't know. If you listen to the French, you would think no, because their whole pattern is drawn around the level of limestone in the soil. We don't have that here, but yet we are able to

achieve a level of acidity that they can't achieve. Believe it or not, even with the flabby, low-acid wines that California produces, the wines for distillation that we use are higher in acid than the Charente wines at the same brix level. So we have to be careful not to get too much sugar and too much alcohol. Will our peak of maturity be thirty-five years? Forty-five? Fifty? We don't know yet. But I'm cautiously optimistic that we have things here that will go half a century."

It seems miraculous that Osocalis is still in business. It faces many of the same challenges confronting Germain-Robin, but it is fully committed to high-end brandy. Its brandies are only distributed in a few states, and its production is so small that it's impossible to imagine a distributor doing the work necessary to get Osocalis's products on shelves. When asked where he sells most of his stuff Farber says, "The right answer is: I don't. It's very hard. I go out and visit a lot of accounts. New York is the most important market in the United States. San Francisco for the most part takes care of itself. Los Angeles is another one of these brand-centric markets. People want to be on the cutting edge, but not really on the cutting edge, because if nobody knows what you're drinking, then you're not cutting edge. You can't be too out in front, and you can't be too far behind. For our type of thing, brandy, and being a very small traditional distiller who's been here for a very long time, we're too out in front. It takes too long to explain us.

"People don't really understand the notion of complexity. If you set out glasses of whisky from, say, Lowlands, Highlands, Campbelltown, Islay, the Hebrides, you'll see the range of flavors you can get from whisky. And that complexity is extremely interesting to a lot of people. When Scotch was dead in the 1970s and they started to market single malts, all of a sudden the consumer said, 'Wow.' Hey, all those are there in Johnnie Walker. You just need to taste and think. But having them separate made it more interesting, and then it made it a game. It was so much easier for people to get their heads around it individually rather than to find it: smoke, *boom*! United States craft distilling, that's today's equivalent of "smoke, boom!" You can pick up whiskies that are smoked, double smoked, triple smoked. There's a lot of smoke. And that smoke is, to some extent, smoke and mirrors. Smoke is a good thing, but not the only thing. You want it as an element. You want to find it. That's the thing about brandy. The minute you find a note in

the early part of your palate, now there's a new one, and then it's gone. As a drinker when you come back to it, it's like, 'Hey wait! It's not the same.' The experience you had before is not the experience you'll have now *because we make it that way.*"

And that subtlety, complexity, *finesse,* and the intention behind creating something with precisely those characteristics is why Farber continues to pursue what might seem like a quixotic quest. He knows enough about distillation to make anything he wants to make, yet he sticks with brandy. In the midst of this boom in craft distilling, someone like Farber should be better known. If "craft" matters, Osocalis XO should be in higher demand than something like, say, Pappy Van Winkle bourbon, which is always highly allocated and gets more expensive every day. (It is one of more than a dozen whiskey brands made in the Buffalo Trace Distillery, just by the way.) Happily, Farber has an appropriately long perspective. He's convinced that the best craft distillers can compete with the big guys, and even with the best producers in Europe, despite their head start. His frustration with the consumer's lack of understanding of what makes a great brown spirit and his aggravation with the poor job the media has done of educating the public and calling out imposters are tempered with an optimism that comes from knowing that what he's making is truly world class. "I hope," he says in conclusion, "we move the conversation more toward what things we can do of great quality—of earth-shatteringly great quality. I think we can do that."

SANTA CRUZ SIDECAR

2 OZ. OSOCALIS RARE ALAMBIC BRANDY

¾ OZ. COINTREAU

¾ OZ. LEMON JUICE

 Combine all ingredients in a cocktail shaker filled with ice and shake until well chilled. Strain into a chilled cocktail glass.

The Shanty, the bar at New York Distilling Company.

CHAPTER 8

BROOKLYN, IT'S NOT JUST FOR HIPSTERS

In the heart of DIY Brooklyn, two regular-looking guys have established one of the country's most well thought out booze-based businesses. If you ignore the industrial neighborhood and the comfortable, well-outfitted bar on the other side of the plate-glass windows, you could be in a small spirit-production facility anywhere.

NEW YORK DISTILLING COMPANY spent $250,000 on its shiny fermentation and distillation equipment, all of it made by Christian Carl, which has been in business in Germany since 1869. Nothing about the operation appears half-baked or patched together; it's elegant in its simplicity. There is a decidedly utilitarian air to the bulk of the space, perhaps because, unlike the gorgeous copper and stainless steel still, the building is leased.

In contrast to many of the recently opened distilleries in the borough, the owners started with a business plan. Their appearances would lead you to expect nothing less. When Allen Katz isn't sporting a beard, he looks more like mild-mannered reporter Clark Kent than a Slow Food evangelist, Director of Mixology & Spirits Education for the New York division of the largest wine and spirits distributor in the United States, and former host of *The Cocktail Hour* on Martha Stewart's radio network. He actually looks like a distiller when he does have the full beard. (It's a magnificently bushy thing that won Katz the 2008 Papa Doble Beard-Off; there doesn't seem to have been a subsequent competition, perhaps in recognition of his follicular invincibility.)

WHERE THE GIRLS AREN'T

An extremely unscientific survey reveals that craft distillers are almost exclusively male, and the vast majority of them sport facial hair. No explanation for this could be found, and none of the stillmen I asked could come up with any persuasive theories. As much as the working conditions at a distillery might resemble those on a submarine, there's always plenty of fresh water (lack of fresh water was the justification for allowing beards on submarines until 1984, when that armed service banned them), and most spirits companies let their employees go home occasionally, so the mystery will have to be left to some intrepid graduate student to unravel.

Cofounder Tom Potter (who looks like he could be Harry Potter's dad) was a founder of Brooklyn's most successful post-Prohibition producer of alcoholic beverages to date, Brooklyn Brewery. As CEO, the former Chemical Bank vice president took the business from labeling bottles in the basement of a Brooklyn brownstone in the mid-eighties to $20 million in sales in 2004, when Potter sold his interest in the brewery to spend more time in his kayak (2012 sales were projected at roughly $40 million). When Potter finally returned to dry land, a mutual friend suggested he talk to Katz about starting a small distillery. Their interests were in synch, and their talents were complimentary: Potter knows booze and finance, and Katz knows booze and evangelism. With the addition of Potter's actual son, Bill, who is the production manager, a plan was hatched.

New York Distilling Company currently has three products on the market, all gins, and all excellent, and its rye whiskey will age until the partners deem it ready. It also has that bar, called The Shanty, with glass separating it from the distillery. As you sip your martini, you can ogle the still on which the gin you're drinking was made. It's the cocktail equivalent of tasting wine at the vineyard or eating at a restaurant with an open kitchen. It makes so much sense it's hard to believe the practice is not more common. There are barriers, of course: some states don't allow it; many—perhaps most—distillers know nothing about running a bar; and building and stocking a bar would add significantly to the already substantial start-up costs facing a distillery.

But it has plenty of benefits, too, the most obvious being that you're very likely to sell more of your product than anything else. And in New York, at least, a distillery can transfer its own product directly from its bonded warehouse to its affiliated bar (after paying all the appropriate taxes, of course), thereby saving it whatever cut the distributor would take. Katz acknowledges the economic benefits, but he has higher goals for the bar. "There are probably 160 to 170 bottles behind the bar now. Three of them are ours. So we're not trying to beat people over the head. If you like Tequila, have Tequila. If you like rum, we have a lovely rum cocktail. Hopefully it's a solid bar, a good place to hang out. Sure, people come in thinking, 'That's the place where they make gin; I've got to taste that. That's great.' Five years from now I suspect it'll be more like, 'That's the bar around the corner. Hey, let's stop by The Shanty.'"

Katz is a born educator—a two-year stint teaching cooking classes in Tuscany, despite having almost no culinary training, led to his involvement with Slow Food—and The Shanty has become one of his classrooms. With no marketing budget, getting noticed on increasingly crowded liquor store and bar shelves is a daunting task. Competing on price is out of the question for a small start-up. So when the bar is closed to the public during the day, Katz puts on occasional comparative tastings and distilling classes for bartenders and other industry professionals, invites them to experiment with his products, and sends them back out in the world with the kinds of stories that will help people connect with the brand.

Having such distinct, and distinctly different, gins certainly makes Katz's task easier. The first recipe the team worked

OPPOSITE: New York Distilling Company cofounders Bill Potter (left),
Tom Potter (center), and Allen Katz (right).

on, with consulting distiller Jason Grizzanti of Warwick Valley Winery & Distillery, was a historical oddity. Navy proof gin—so-called because beginning in the early nineteenth century it was made for the British Royal Navy at a proof (114) that would not render gunpowder useless if gin casks broke and soaked the explosive—is rare today even in the United Kingdom and, until New York Distilling came along, unheard of in the United States. Keeping its powder lit was not the motivation behind reintroducing a gin that was 57 percent alcohol by volume. Katz describes the company's philosophy as trying to be "purposefully different." The navy strength gin, which is called Perry's Tot after Matthew Perry, the commandant of the nearby Brooklyn Navy Yard from 1841 to 1843, fits that bill. It also appeals to modern bartenders because high-proof spirits have more flavor, allowing for the addition of other bold flavors to a cocktail without losing the taste of the spirit. Navy strength gin could be seen as little more than a novelty, but several small distilleries have recently released one, and established UK brand Plymouth has begun to bring in its overproof bottling; it doesn't do things just to be different. That's not Katz's aim, either.

"We're not trying to be esoteric," he says. "We're looking for the places within the realm of products that we really love where we can add to the conversation. In gin, navy strength does that automatically."

Banking on a niche product to tide the company over until its whiskey is ready was one level of risk too high for the firmly terrestrial partners. Katz readily admits that there's been plenty of uncertainty along the way.

OPPOSITE: Two of the three gins made by New York Distilling Company.

"The stress level creeps up a little bit. You think: 'If the navy strength gin is too strong, let's have an additional offering.' Our nimbleness allows us some creativity. So we made a more contemporary style gin." To differentiate it from Perry's Tot, Katz bottles it at a more approachable 88 proof, and the botanicals are a combination of traditional (juniper, coriander, lemon, and orange peel) and less traditional (elderberry and hibiscus). He calls it Dorothy Parker American Gin after the famed satirist, poet, social activist, and gin lover. There isn't really any such thing as American gin, but the phrase lets the consumer know that this isn't in the style of London dry gin. Now that everyone's a critic, and everyone's critique is instantaneously broadcast through blogs, Twitter, Facebook, Yelp, and other platforms, the term may also insulate the gin from harsh, snap judgments. After all, if you don't like it as much as, say, Tanqueray, well it's not trying to be like Tanqueray. The label

asks you to judge it on its own terms, not based on preconceptions of what gin should taste like.

Katz adds that "we called it American gin in deference and respect to the world and history of gin. A decade from now, twenty-five years from now, we'll see what contemporary gins have lasted, and maybe there will be a recognized category called 'American gin.'"

Katz made up another spirit category, New-Netherland gin, to describe his Chief Gowanus, which is made with New York Distilling Company rye redistilled with juniper berries and hops and aged for three months in oak. It was developed with the help of cocktail historian David Wondrich, who found the recipe in *The Practical Distiller*, which was published in 1809. In *Imbibe!*, Wondrich's indispensable book about classic mixology and its Zeus, Jerry Thomas, Wondrich argues persuasively that gin cocktails of the early to mid-nineteenth century would have been made with Holland-style gin until "the American public's

turn to lighter cocktails in the 1880s" and "the rise of the Dry Martini, in the 1890s," which led to London dry gin displacing the "richer Dutch style."

The other spirit that New York Distilling Company is producing is rye whiskey. It won't be released until it's ready, and there's no way to know exactly when that will be—as Katz likes to say when asked, "How long is a piece of string?"—but the goal is to have it on the market in October 2014. Rye has undergone a bit of a boom in recent years—the Distilled Spirits Council of the United States says rye sales have seen a 20 percent annual increase over the last few years at a time when the industry has been seeing just under 5 percent annual growth—but that's not why Katz decided to make it.

"We love bourbon, love drinking it; we're big fans," he says. "But as much as we love bourbon, we just didn't feel there was a lot we could add to the conversation. So partly because of our passion for history—cultural history and cocktail history—our focus is on American rye. For one thing, rye was a major crop in New York two hundred plus years ago. I thought it would be nice to work with some farms in New York and create a strong context of the place of this product. So we source all of our rye from a farmer up near Seneca Lake, in the Finger Lakes. Our corn all comes from upstate New York. That's not uncommon these days. People are getting local grains. But before we even had our still, we were already investing in agriculture. We'd already paid for plantings of rye before we were even operational."

With the gin and the bar as revenue streams, Katz has been able to avoid the small-barrel issue altogether. Almost all of New York Distilling Company's whiskey is aging in

OPPOSITE: The still at the New York Distilling Company.

fifty-three-gallon barrels. It has a few thirty-gallon barrels as well, but those were bought in a moment of exuberance in the spirit of experimentation.

"Delivered to us door to door, a five-gallon barrel costs a hundred and fifty dollars," says Katz. "Delivered to us door to door, a full barrel costs two hundred. So okay, yes, I could get more color and some quick intensity of flavor, and I could potentially get a product out faster, and that would mean a revenue stream that I don't have right now. But the most important factor is taste. We've tasted a lot of great whiskey that's come out of fifty-three-gallon barrels. You always take advantage of what's come before you. We've tasted products from all parts of the world in different size barrels. It's not to say in any way that the small-barrel products are bad; many of them are quite lovely. What I like most about the taste of a longer aging process is the nuance that comes out of those full-size barrels. It's a potentially precarious position to take because as a start-up we've incurred debt."

Another thing the company is working on is, in fact, a bit of a novelty. Rock and rye became a popular bottled "medicinal preparation" during Prohibition; before that it was primarily found as an early bottled cocktail. Saloonkeepers would put rock candy in a bottle of rye along with various fruits and herbs. What probably started as a way to improve the flavor of an aggressively spicy, hot spirit quickly became a go-to cough remedy. Writing in volume 10 of *The Memphis Medical Monthly*, published in 1890, Dr. T.A. Atchison, professor of Materia Medica and Therapeutics at the University of Nashville and Vanderbilt University, admits that "Bronchial irritations and laryngeal irritations attended by a harassing cough, are . . . soothed by this agent." He goes on to criticize doctors for prescribing rock and rye for these maladies because, "the saloon-keepers have 'caught-on' and . . . if you will take your position in front of the doors of these gilded saloons about the city, and quietly observe, you will see a gentleman coming along the street; when he gets within twenty yards of the door of the saloon he commences coughing, and he puts his hand over his chest with an agonized expression and slips in the door and takes some 'rock and rye.' And every time he goes by a saloon he is seized with a cough."

More than half a century later, as Eric Felten pointed out in a 2009 *Wall Street Journal* piece on the concoction, Dr. Thomas G. Ward, a prominent Johns Hopkins virologist, was asked what he recommended for the common cold. Felten quotes Ward as saying, "Personally, my favorite treatment is old Maryland Rock and Rye."

Today we know that there is no cure for the common cold, and the drugstore shelves bulge with a dizzying array of symptom-controllers at increasingly outrageous prices. (Most of them contain the exact same active ingredients despite the differing claims made on their packages.) Liquor is much less popular for medicinal applications today, but I'm not sure why: rock and rye tastes so much better than Robitussin. Nonetheless, Katz is obviously not looking to capitalize on the phlegm-afflicted. His love of history and the recognition that he could use some of that young rye that hasn't aged long enough to be bottled—and get some revenue from it—led him to develop a rock and rye recipe.

"A lot of this boutique industry at the moment is looking for novelties," says Katz. "Is there an interesting tea? Is there an interesting flavor that's popular in the beverage world that we can mimic in an alcoholic beverage? In a liqueur? Is there something that's indigenous to a particular locale or region, and can we capitalize on that local story? I look at rock and rye as a healthy novelty. We're trying to make things that we can offer for a reasonable price, but it's labor intensive and the start-up costs are high. Part of trying to offer things at a fair price is telling the story of how things are made. There's so much interest in looking back to ingredients that are more or less defunct that I think rock and rye can have some popularity. Rock and rye traditionally was young, rough rye whiskey that was tempered with a little bit of rock candy sugar. Ours will be a fruited rock and rye with tart sour cherries from upstate New York. We're not doing that out of some sense of ethical obligation; we like having that relationship with a grower. Our rye farmer comes down with his kids from upstate, and they have a ball here. It's another piece in the drink chain from one entrepreneur to the next. It's saying, 'I like and value these things, and I hope that other people will too.'

"With all the very serious conversation about whiskey—the evaluation and philosophical contemplation—rock and rye has some of those attributes, but it's also just fun. And it's also fun for us to be able to reclaim part of something uniquely American because we have a distillery with a bar attached to it. Once upon a time, bars around the city had their own house rock and rye. It's not meant to be highbrow, but we want to tell the artisan, craftsmanship story of how we make the product. It does allow us to introduce a little bit of rye to the marketplace and slowly become recognized as a whiskey-producing distilling company. It says, 'Hey, we're gonna have more rye whiskey, and in time, when we think it's right and ready, we'll release straight rye whiskey.'"

It remains to be seen how that rye will taste when it is deemed ready. Although New York State was never a major rye-producing state, lots of it was made in neighboring Pennsylvania and nearby Maryland and Virginia. Southern distillers claim their climate is the only one suitable to aging whiskies, but they would say that. Katz feels the New York climate is not radically different than the traditional bourbon and rye regions, and that aging in Brooklyn will not limit the whiskies' quality potential. But of course he would say that.

"Yes, Kentucky summers are a little bit longer, so you get a few more hot days. And I love these 100-degree days. You smell it. You smell it! It's exciting. No, they don't have the amount of snow we have, but they certainly have harsh temperatures in the winter in Kentucky. So I don't know."

And this, as much as anything, is what's so exciting about a small distiller trying to do things the right way. Nobody knows what the end result will be, but standing on the shoulders of all the great distillers who've come before, looking for ways of doing things that fit a modern, low-impact, locally focused philosophy, people like Katz and Potter *père e fils* have a chance to make something truly great.

SAUVETAGE

Courtesy of The Shanty, Williamsburg, Brooklyn

1 OZ. DOROTHY PARKER AMERICAN GIN
1 OZ. CARPANO ANTICA FORMULA VERMOUTH
½ OZ. AMERSAUVAGE GENTIAN LIQUEUR (BITTERMAN'S)
½ OZ. FRESH GRAPEFRUIT JUICE

Combine ingredient in a cocktail shaker filled with ice. Shake and strain into a chilled cocktail glass.

White whiskey is my least favorite craft distilling category. I object to its usual mischaracterization as "moonshine"—if it's made legally, in a licensed distillery, it's not moonshine, it's just unaged whiskey. The sensory side of my problem is that it's just not as interesting as aged whiskey. As a product you can buy in a liquor store, it feels like a fad, and by definition a fad is something that loses popularity as fast as it gained it. I also have a nagging suspicion that some of the white whiskies on the market are the result of distillers trying to make something vodka-like but stopping short of vodka's neutrality because it's difficult—and expensive—to achieve (and almost impossible in a pot still). Still, I have had some white whiskies that I thought were pretty good, though none of them seemed like a finished product.

One of the really good ones comes from Brooklyn's **KINGS COUNTY DISTILLERY**. But lest you think this is some trust-fund hipster art project, Colin Spoelman is from Kentucky. He used to buy moonshine. So he's the real deal. Well, maybe a post-modern version of the real deal. "I grew up in a dry county in Kentucky so when I was in high school we'd go to the bootlegger before our 'campouts,'" recalls Spoelman. "The bootlegger I normally went to would go to Virginia and buy Zima, or whatever the package store in Virginia was selling. There was a woman in town who sold moonshine, but I wouldn't say it was a part of my culture growing up. Going back later, I developed a curiosity about moonshine."

Spoelman's curiosity led him to bring back some of the actual illicit spirit (and not Zima) after a trip home. His friends in Brooklyn liked it, and he began to think about a little side business. "I thought maybe it'd be cool to buy a bunch of it and bring it back to New York, but that also seemed like maybe a terrible idea. Trying to go through the Holland Tunnel with a trunk full of moonshine didn't sound very bright." And for most people that would have been the end of it. Running illegal booze from Kentucky to New York would be dumb, so move on. And Spoelman did just that. He started *making* moonshine. Because, what? That's less illegal?

He got himself a still, started making moonshine that he says was "pretty awful," and asked people what they thought. Some of the responses he recalls were, "I like what you're doing." "It's a cool idea." And "I would drink if it you made it taste good." So Spoelman spent a few years distilling on his porch (because nobody would ever notice that?), trying to get something that he thought matched the refinement of his audience's taste. At a certain point he felt he'd achieved that, and that's when his cofounder, David  Haskell, stepped in and said, "I think there's a business here. Let's see what it takes to get licensed. It can't be that hard." As Spoelman says, "It turns out it is that hard. But on the other hand, it wasn't that hard because New York State had just changed its laws and we had a great lawyer. We weren't trying to do that much. We just wanted to take the operation that was on the porch, multiply it by 4, and set up a one-room operation. We didn't have to raise a lot of money, didn't have to renovate a building; it was just 'let's see what happens.'"

What happened was they moved into a building that already housed a jerky company, a wallpaper company, and a recording studio. Their space was on the second floor, which isn't necessarily the best place for a distillery. Spoelman is a bit more blunt. "Being on the second floor was really stupid because everything leaked every time we spilled, and we spill a lot. But we were able to get the business going. We quickly reached the amount of stores and bars we could service, so we knew we wanted to expand. The license gives you a tasting room, which is a big advantage, so we wanted a place that had a lot of foot traffic. On the flip side of that, we were way off the beaten track, and we were getting three hundred visitors a day in a place where people couldn't find us. And we didn't have anything for them to see. They'd show up, and we'd say, 'Wait in the hallway,

and we'll bring you into this little room and talk about it and then you can go back to the hallway.' There was nothing to tour. But people came. One group was from the Brooklyn Navy Yard, and they asked if we'd thought about moving to the Navy Yard. We said no, and no, we don't want to move to the Navy Yard. It's not very open, there's no foot traffic, it's hard to get to. But they showed us this building. It's not far from the train; it has a yard. They gave us a price range, and it was about what we were going to pay to be seven stops into Brooklyn in a corrugated metal and cinder block warehouse. So it seemed like a no-brainer."

The 1905 brick Paymaster Building is about twenty times the size of the distillery's original space, and it's gorgeous. It may have required more work than the warehouse would have, but it's an extremely inviting space. The main floor is dedicated to fermentation and distillation, while the second floor has the tasting room and barrel storage. In February 2013, two new stills, which were designed by the third partner in Kings County Distillery, Nicole Austin (she studied chemical engineering in college), arrived from Scotland, effectively increasing the company's capacity by a factor of 10 once they are producing. The stills—one holds 264 gallons the other holds 170—will replace the five 26-gallon stills that replaced the five 8-gallon stills Kings County started with. The new fermenters are unusual in that they're made of wood, by one of the last remaining manufacturers of rooftop water tanks, Isseks Brothers. As a result of these upgrades, Kings County Distillery will go from producing about a liter of 73 percent alcohol per run to somewhere around 15 gallons per shift.

OPPOSITE: Kings County, New York City's oldest operating whiskey distillery, was founded 105 years after its building was constructed.

The expanded production may also make it possible for Spoelman to try making a single malt, something he has thought about but never attempted. "It's a little weird to do in America because you can't call it Scotch," he says. "It'd be an interesting experiment. If we were to try it, I'd like to smoke the malt here and do our own take on it."

In addition to the corn-based white whiskey (made from a mashbill of 80 percent corn and 20 percent malted barley) and bourbon (75 percent corn and 25 percent malted barley), Kings County Distillery has made small amounts of brandy and a tiny amount of rye. The company also infuses its white whiskey with cacao husks from the incomparable Mast Brothers, a bean-to-bar chocolate producer based in nearby Williamsburg, Brooklyn. But the focus will always be on corn-based spirits. Spoelman describes his white whiskey as "way less corny than some of the other corn whiskies." I would agree with that characterization. In fact, it struck me as having the refinement of an eau de vie. Spoelman feels that this "has a lot to do with the type of corn we're using. Of the ones we tried, this one has the most earthy, most complex, and the least corny flavor."

That corn comes from Lakeview Organic Grain, a farm in central New York State. "A lot of the New York distilleries are using an heirloom corn," Spoelman continues. "Another thing, despite what's on some labels, there's no way you can make a whiskey with all corn. You need some sort of malted grain to be able to extract the sugar from the starch. In our case that's barley. The barley comes from the United Kingdom. It's a particular strain that was bred for whiskey production. If you have all corn, you have to be adding some enzymes. What the enzymes do is they give it a really specific narrow band of flavor, which can be great. If it's a wheat whiskey, you get this baking-bread quality. But what works well for wheat doesn't necessarily work all that well for corn. You get this funny popcorn flavor that isn't all that appropriate to whiskey. The major ingredient here that's broadening that band of flavor is the enzymes that are in the barley."

The bourbon is aged in small barrels for a relatively long time—between twelve and twenty-four months, depending on the season, how full the barrels are, where in the aging room the barrels are stored, and variations in char levels. The result is quite a woody whiskey, but after a few minutes in the glass it softens a bit, revealing spices, chocolate, and some sweetness. Spoelman is experimenting with a range of barrel sizes but feels careful distillation makes it possible to use smaller barrels without sacrificing quality. Industrial distillers don't have to aim as high as their craft brethren because they know they can let the longer time in large barrels remove problems created during fermentation or distillation. Many large bourbon producers use continuous stills, which are more efficient but create a less-flavorful spirit, whereas the little guys have to make conservative—and expensive—heads and tails cuts knowing that their whiskey is going to be bottled and sold young. For big producers, age and quality probably have a pretty strong correlation. Spoelman feels that craft distillers are changing that equation. "I'm not convinced that age should be the measure of a bourbon—it's not designed to be aged like Scotch. I think once we move to bigger barrels we'll be making a compromise. I think small barrels are great, and more people would use them if they were cost effective. Fifty-gallon barrels were a cost-savings measure once upon a time. If you were buying whiskey in the Middle Ages you were not getting a fifty-gallon barrel. You were probably getting a cask for your castle. We're looking very narrowly at history to say that the fifty-gallon barrel is the gold standard. That's my perspective." It's also the perspective of Orlin Sorensen, of Woodinville Whiskey Co. (see Chapter 9), who says, "That became the standard when Independent Stave opened up in 1912. Their massive production made that size so inexpensive—a fifty-three-gallon barrel costs less than an eight-gallon barrel!" It seems clear that in the mid-nineteenth century the standard barrel size for whiskey storage and transportation was forty gallons, and it's likely that the size increase was motivated by economics.

Spoelman sees the focus on age and barrel size as a bit of a relic. The question of how to value a whiskey—or just about anything else—is complex and mutable. At the moment, age and scarcity seem to drive demand in the whiskey market. "I think how people understand what makes good whiskey will change," Spoelman says. "I think it'll be more about the quality of the distillation, because I think a lot of the Kentucky bourbons are not all that well distilled. I think they're well aged.

Right now microdistillers are not able to age their stuff well, and the big distillers have so much production they can't distill their stuff well. Someone is going to figure out how to be in the middle, and my guess is it'll be Tuthilltown [see Chapter 2]. There are a couple of Kentucky distilleries, like Buffalo Trace, that are big but have some smaller equipment dedicated to special production. But you certainly can't get organic whiskey out of Kentucky. Not to say that is necessarily better, but the ingredients make a difference, and when the ingredients come from hybrid corn grown for yield, not for flavor, surely that has an effect on the whiskey. In Kentucky they tell you it's the limestone water that makes all the difference. It doesn't make any difference at all. There's very little of that water that gets through the distillation process. It may make their mashes more productive, but in terms of flavor, no. And they're shoving in all these lab-synthesized enzymes. Hey, blast it with enzymes. If people can't tell the difference, who cares? But it's a different approach to the process than small distilleries have, and that approach certainly has an impact on the flavor."

Most craft distillers aren't able to quit their day jobs. A surprising number have more-interesting-than-average day jobs, but Daric Schlesselman, owner of **VAN BRUNT STILLHOUSE**, in Red Hook, Brooklyn, might win the prize. He works at *The Daily Show*, where he's been an editor since 2001. Schlesselman says he was looking for something completely different to balance his everyday work. "The television business is so ephemeral. It's all ideas—it's a moment in time, and then it's gone and it's done. I come from a family of farmers, and I have this in my bones: the need to do and make and have something tangible. The development of my interest was very organic. I went from enjoying the do-it-yourself mentality of making cider and beer and then to making my own spirits. Distilling is an agricultural act—sort of a mixture of cooking and gardening—and it's a great meeting of craft and science and alchemy. The fermentation part of it never ceases to amaze me. To open up that lid and see that magic happening, it's like being a rancher and a gardener and a cook."

And like ranching, gardening, and cooking, distilling at this level is not a way to make a quick buck. Or maybe any bucks. For some people, the satisfaction of making something is reward enough. Schlesselman has children though, so the distillery has to be more than a hobby. And he says he's in it for the long haul. "I want to have a small business, and I would like to give this to my children. I have no idea if my children will want it, but that's one of my motivations."

Until his kids get a little older, it's just him, his wife, and one employee, and they're distilling about fifty gallons a week. Intriguingly, production is seasonal. In the summer they make rum, and in the winter they make whiskey. Schlesselman is also a grappa lover, and he's making that rustic spirit from winemaking leftovers sourced from local wineries. (Brooklyn actually has a couple of wineries, though no commercial vineyards that I'm aware of, and Schlesselman also has gotten pomace from Lieb Cellars on Long Island.)

When I visited Van Brunt Stillhouse, in the summer of 2012, Schlesselman had recently gotten a shipment of sugar, and he was making rum. Getting sugar sounds like a simple matter, but he had made a miscalculation. "I thought that sugar was just a commodity and that you could call up on the phone and order it. My mistake was that I chose the best sugar I could find—naturally processed, organic sugar cane. It's an Indian, non-industrial version of sugar called *jaggery*. They dry it in

OPPOSITE: Daric Schlesselman, owner of the Van Brunt Stillhouse, in Red Hook, Brooklyn, has his hand in every aspect of his business.

the sun. I called the guy up and negotiated the sugar. Then I called him in October, and he said, 'Okay, we'll deliver in May.' I was like, 'Huh?' It turns out he sells all his sugar before it gets made, and it gets made between January and April. So I was out of luck until this came in."

There's no doubt that what Schlesselman is doing is craft, and like everyone who puts as much effort into making spirits as he does, he's critical of those who buy an industrial product and craft-wash it. "I don't have a lot of respect for people who are buying somebody else's mass-produced product and then saying that they're a small business and therefore they're craft. But one thing I definitely have learned to respect is that getting to this point is Sisyphean. If you have to do something to get to this point that's different than the way I would do it, I have no place to criticize you for it. The way that I do business is I get the best raw materials I can and I distill them in the best possible way and age them in the best way I can. That to me is craft."

THE SUPERFUND
(AKA IMPROVED GOWANUS COCKTAIL)

Courtesy David Wondrich, Author, Brooklyn, NY

2 OZ. CHIEF GOWANUS NEW-NETHERLAND GIN

1 BARSPOON RICH SIMPLE SYRUP (SEE RECIPE BELOW)

1 BARSPOON PIERRE FERRAND DRY ORANGE CURAÇAO

2 DASHES FEE BROS. WHISKEY BARREL BITTERS

1 DASH (FROM A DASHER BOTTLE) ABSINTHE

Combine all ingredients in a mixing glass filled with ice, and stir until well chilled. Strain into a chilled cocktail glass. Garnish with a lemon twist.

RICH SIMPLE SYRUP

2 CUPS WATER
1 CUP GRANULATED SUGAR

In a saucepan, stir together water and sugar. Bring to a gentle boil and reduce heat to a simmer, Stir until sugar is dissolved, about 3 minutes. Remove from heat. When cool, transfer syrup to a container with a lid and store in the refrigerator. Syrup will keep for 3 to 4 weeks.

Jake Norris of Laws Whiskey House.

CHAPTER 9

DOING IT THE RIGHT WAY

One of America's most successful craft whiskey distillers is also one of its most complicated. He's a man with a deep and unwavering moral code, but if you want to work with him, be prepared: one of your job interviews may require you to go out with him and get wasted, possibly at a strip club. He's a sharp businessman, but he seems to have been unprepared when a larger company was attracted to his distillery's success. His car is, to be kind, utilitarian—his stove cost more than his ride and is the heart of what he calls his "bitchin' kitchen." The day we met he never stopped moving as he worked for the three hours we spent talking about everything from bubble plates to beheading chickens, but I never felt that his attention wasn't focused completely on our discussion.

From the day it opened, in March 2004, Jake Norris was the head distiller at Stranahan's Colorado Whiskey. The history of the distillery has been told well in various places, including Max Watman's *Chasing the White Dog*, but the nuts and bolts of it are that a volunteer firefighter named Jess Graber had been making whiskey illegally in Woody Creek, Colorado, near Aspen, and wanted to go legit, with the help of a partner, George Stranahan. At the time, Norris was tending bar in Denver and doing some illicit home distilling of his own. He and Graber had independently come to the conclusion that rather than make their own wash, they would have it made by a local brewery. Given the number of excellent craft brewers in Denver, that they would both hit on Flying Dog (founded, not incidentally, by George Stranahan) at around the same time has to be counted as one of the great examples of synchronicity, right up there with the discoveries of calculus, oxygen, and evolution.

When the two met, Norris sketched for Graber the still he wanted to build, and Graber told Norris about the Vendome still he was going to buy. You guessed it; they were the same design. Of course, as Watman writes, "Jake's was a beer keg, and Jess's 165 gallons. Jake's was fabricated and rigged; and Jess's was solid copper with beautiful brass fittings and portals and adjustable plates in the column. Regardless, the two stills were based upon the same idea."

When Graber and Stranahan offered him a job, Norris seized the opportunity to do on a large scale what he'd been dreaming about doing on a modest scale. In fact, he seized it so hard he basically squeezed out the rest of his life. "In eight years," he says, "we went from a couple of guys in an old warehouse to a $15 million company. That's how everybody looks at it, but everything I did was about that. I didn't just go out to dinner; I talked to every bartender, every server, the manager. I brought a bottle out of my car to sample. It used to drive girlfriends mad because I was never off the clock. I hadn't taken a vacation in eight years because that had been my everything. Stranahan's was more important than the girl I was dating, than vacations; it was more important than just about everything. I was my own slave driver—I did it to myself—it was my priority."

Rumors surfaced in 2010 that Stranahan's was on the block, but it wasn't until the year-end that an announcement was made about a deal with Proximo, which had earlier purchased Hangar One vodka from the Germain-Robin–St. George partnership.

Though Norris was an owner, he was very much a minority owner, so his options were limited. His investment was in sweat and blood, and he was certainly rewarded for it. But how do you put a dollar figure on eight years of life that you'll never get back? It may have been difficult for Ansley Coale, Jörg Rupf, and Lance Winters to give up Hangar One, but if it was, the reasons would mostly have been economic. It's hard to imagine developing a deep emotional attachment to a vodka.

As idealistic as Norris is, he is by no means starry-eyed. Nor is he blind to his good fortune. "I got to do something that I never expected I'd be able to do, and it was an unqualified success. It totally exceeded all our expectations: people's reception, critics' reception, distribution, financially, the speed at which we were able to grow, how receptive the market was. None of us could've anticipated that it was going to go as well as it did."

Hangar One vodkas, Tuthilltown's Hudson whiskies, and Stranahan's Colorado Whiskey are three of the most successful craft spirits brands, and all were snapped up by larger companies. But knowing that he was on the leading edge of what is inevitably going to be a period of consolidation, mimicking to a degree what happened in craft brewing twenty years ago, probably doesn't make the impact any easier to take.

An interesting change has taken place since Proximo bought Stranahan's Colorado Whiskey. The old branding featured "Colorado" most prominently. Today the word is gone from the distillery building and much smaller on the bottle. Kristin Forsch, Stranahan's brand ambassador, explains that the change was made because "people come to town and they go to their hotel bar and ask for 'Colorado whiskey.' Now that there are twenty-five other microdistilleries, they're getting Leopold,

OPPOSITE: The sign used to say "Stranahan's Colorado Whiskey."

they're getting Breckenridge, so we had to change it so people wouldn't get confused." It's unclear why someone asking for "Colorado whiskey" today is more likely to get Stranahan's now that "Colorado" has been minimized on the label, but perhaps with a large marketing campaign the company will be able to make "Stranahan's" a more powerful brand name.

For the more cynical among us, however, it's hard not to wonder if the company is hedging its bets just in case it decides in the future to blend in something not made in the Rockies to meet demand or move production somewhere else. Though Norris might say it's no longer his problem, I suspect if Stranahan's ever became less than 100 percent Colorado made, he would be saddened. For that matter, I suspect his former colleagues who stayed with the company would be saddened, too, but they may not have the financial security to take the moral high ground as he did.

CONSUMING THE LITTLE GUYS

There will be more mergers and acquisitions, as well as spirits produced by industrial distillers designed to capitalize on the increasing interest in craft products (just as Budweiser makes Shock Top and Coors makes Blue Moon to compete with Belgian-style witbier). If whiskey companies like Templeton, WhistlePig, and High West, all of which bottle excellent whiskies blended from purchased stock, haven't established a number at which they will walk away, they should do so soon, or it will be too late. They have hit on a business model that worked well at the moment they came to market, but as mature whiskey stocks are depleted and as the large companies that own them catch on to the craft phenomenon, the model will fall apart. No matter how loudly those small guys protest that they're only selling blended whiskey until their own distillery is fully operational and their spirit has aged sufficiently, the likelihood that the old will flow seamlessly into the new—both in terms of flavor profile and inventory—seems slim. These are "craft distilleries." (Really they are craft blenders, but unfortunately none have embraced the term. Instead, they prefer to tout their "master distiller" or the quality of their local grain, even though they may not have sold anything they have distilled and none of it was made from grain they bought.) They have every intention of making their whiskey, but it's hard to imagine how they'll pull it off. Breckenridge Distillery claims to be in the process of transitioning from all purchased whiskey to at least partially homemade stock, and Oola Distillery, based in Seattle, blends a combination of purchased and produced spirits. Oola's owner, Kirby Kallas-Lewis, says that as time goes on he's "using less and less sourced, so at some point we probably will not use any." He adds that "for me it's all about the flavor profile. If some sourced improves things, I have nothing against using a small amount as we go forward." Of course, labeling laws allow all of these whiskies to be bottled and labeled in such a way that the provenance of the liquid inside is rather opaque. Some producers choose transparency; others, perhaps fearing that their "local" marketing message will be diluted by the knowledge that the whiskey is not local, do not. WhistlePig, for example, has "Vermont" on the front label three times; there are only thirteen other words not related to proof or age. WhistlePig is a delicious rye. But it's Canadian rye. That information can be found, in tiny type, on the back label, but it seems unlikely that many consumers would ever get that far.

Norris knows full well why Proximo came after the whiskey he poured his heart into: "We did a little bit too good of a job, and we attracted the big guys. I didn't turn the check down, but that wasn't what I wanted—that wasn't what I was trying to do. That's what the investors wanted to do. I can't really fault them; people risked money for reward, and that was their reward. Corporate America and myself, we don't share the same goals and values. I never want an accountant making a craftsman's decision. They get paid based on how much more cheaply they can do something and with how many fewer people. That's not how I work. How I work is you start with a goal to make the best whiskey possible and you do whatever it takes to achieve that."

He stayed on as long as he could, hoping that the New Jersey–based company would be true to its word when it said it had, as an unnamed executive told Denver's alternative weekly *Westworld*, "no intention of changing anything," and "We just want to make what they've done bigger." Norris lasted about eight months, but he probably would have left sooner if it hadn't been so important to him that his barrel manager, Rob Dietrich, have every chance to succeed him as distiller. "I wouldn't trade the experience for anything," says Norris. "It was wonderful, but I'm also glad I left when I did. It was a very good decision for me as far as being true to myself, being true to my convictions, and not accepting that gradual moral erosion that occurs in that cash-heavy environment where if you just play ball there's

all these wonderful rewards. I was lucky enough that I was an owner so I wasn't financially crippled and I could make the right decisions. I can't get up on my high horse—if you have kids to feed, I'm not going to criticize—but I designed my life so I could be high speed, low drag, low commitment. As a result I had the luxury of making these completely moral decisions."

Proximo may turn out to be a good steward of the Stranahan's brand. Perhaps the quality of the whiskey won't be compromised, and the company certainly will employ more people. And maybe, having invested heavily in Denver, it will be a great corporate citizen. But for Norris, even if those outcomes are within the realm of possibility, the early signs were not good. "They told me, 'If you stick with this, you're going to be the face of this brand. You'll do every TV commercial, every magazine. For the rest of your life all you'll have to do is fly into a city, shake hands, and drink whiskey.'"

But that wasn't the life he wanted, and initially he tried to push back. "I'd go on these diatribes in meetings, and they'd tell me, 'This is the real world.' But I didn't see why we couldn't make something I'm proud of that's legitimate and honest and that takes care of the people that work on it, that makes an effort to take care of its community. Charities, community events, local police organizations, firefighters: that's our community. If I'm just taking money out of it, that's not sustainable. Yeah, I'm buying grain locally so it's not being trucked as far, and everything I'm using is non-GMO, but beyond that, sustainability is being part of your community so your community sustains you.

"I knew I was leaving after the third or fourth production meeting when we sat down and they had me run numbers. 'Do we need brewers? Couldn't we just take this recipe and have it produced in Lynchburg?' which is where all Templeton's rye comes from. I stayed as long as I could stomach it out of a sense of responsibility. I made this whiskey; I'm going to give them the tools to keep it good if they choose to. And I really wanted to make sure Rob was set up. He put in a lot of good work, and he earned his spot; he was a shoo-in for the job. He's also more suited to that environment than I was."

Dietrich and Norris are still friends and clearly respect each other, and not just because when they met they both were riding alternative-fuel motorcycles. Norris's was powered by the discarded heads from distillation: Dietrich's, made from a Czechoslovakian bike mated to the diesel engine from an old cement mixer, ran on vegetable oil. (They also share a history in the music business so it's possible that hearing loss is a contributing factor in their friendship.)

Having stayed long enough to feel comfortable leaving, Norris then did the only sensible thing. He took several months off, including a month with his family, which he says was "the most time I'd spent with my family since high school." Jake's father, Tony, is a singer and storyteller who has performed at folk festivals, cowboy poetry gatherings, and storytelling festivals around the country.

In addition to music making, and the general driving-each-other-crazy that all families engage in when they're together, Jake built an earthen oven in the backyard, something he says he'd wanted to do for a long time, and baked bread and pizzas in it. Then he went off to pursue another longtime interest. "I had the time to do whatever I wanted," he says. "I always wanted to learn knifesmithing, so I spent three months training under a guy who makes samurai swords. I don't want

THE BABY WITH THE
BRANCH WATER

There are some wonderful stories on Tony Norris's website
(tonynorris.com), including one that takes place near Midkiff,
West Virginia, in 1973. Tony and his wife, Sue, were living there
on the farm of a former moonshiner named Almon Lewis.

> We had an acre and a half in bloody butcher corn, whip-poor-
> will peas, velvet beans and fat, red mortgage lifter tomatoes.
>
> One frosty September morning, we harvested sleds full of
> winter squash and pumpkins and tucked them into the base of
> the shocks we'd formed of the cornstalks. In the afternoon we
> drove to an abandoned apple orchard fifteen miles away and col-
> lected a winter's worth of red and golden delicious apples and a
> half dozen varieties I couldn't name. Sue went into labor on the
> way home and that night Jacob Almon Norris was born.
>
> When Jacob was just two weeks old I carried him horseback
> around the eighty acres to show him his new home. At the head
> of the holler, we stopped at a spring that ran from the base of a
> giant black walnut. The numerous shards of broken fruit jars
> scattered about confirmed this as Almon's favored still site. I
> filled my mouth with the cool sweet water and dribbled a little
> into Jacob's open mouth.

Tony Norris wrote that story in May 2006, a week after
being present at the tapping of the first cask of Jacob Almon
Norris's Stranahan's Colorado Whiskey. No Hollywood script
editor would allow such a far-fetched plot twist.

to make weapons; I want to make chefs' knives, but I know the finest swords ever made were the *katana*, the Japanese samurai swords, and I wanted to take that technology and make cooking knives. I've got a mildly obsessive personality. When I get involved in something, I don't just casually follow it on Twitter or something. I immerse myself in it, and I'm not satisfied until I have a certain level of mastery. Of course, you're never really a master of anything. But being a nerd, I went straight for the oldest, old school, most hardcore thing. Right off the bat the knives I enjoyed producing the most were all forged steel. They come out all dinged up from the hammer, and they're all black. People who don't know knives are like, 'Eww, is that one rusty?' Then you have to explain it: 'This shows you that I was able to forge it; it's not ground. This is actually forged into the shape that it's in; it's not stock removal. It wasn't forged thicker and then ground down.' I still make them shiny if people want them shiny."

Making knives can certainly be a lucrative trade, but it takes years to develop the skills and establish a reputation. And in the middle of this boom in craft distilling, Norris's experience was in great demand (and he was practically baptized in a moonshiner's creek, for crying out loud). "To be honest," he says, "I wasn't sure I was going to come back to spirits. But I realized I didn't want to be defined by that one success. I didn't want to leave open the possibility that I was a one-hit wonder or that I just got lucky or something. I started consulting because I could, and because it was lucrative, and I ended up meeting some really passionate people who reminded me why I got into it to begin with. I also came into contact with a whole bunch of people that were in it for what I considered to be exactly the wrong reason: people who were just jumping in the boat. These are the guys who are bottling [neutral grain spirit] and calling it vodka that they distilled; these are the guys who are bottling Heaven Hill and calling it their own, and that's just not how I roll.

"But among the people who are in it for the right reasons was Al [Laws]. It's rare to meet someone who's so passionate, honest, and who's doing it for the right reasons. After consulting with him for a few months he said, 'If you want, I have a spot for you.' We agreed that at least for the first three years I'd still be able to consult because I'd started relationships and I didn't feel like it would be fair to bail on people I'd committed to. So I'm seeing through projects that I've started, but this is where I'm committed. I'm here four days a week, and I consult three days a week. And when I find time in the schedule, I make knives."

OPPOSITE: Knifemaking is the exit strategy for
Laws Whiskey House distiller Jake Norris.

Al Laws moved from Brooklyn to Denver, in 2007, with his wife, Marianne, and their two children. Al is a financial analyst specializing in the oil industry, and he has a wide-ranging whiskey collection that Norris describes as "phenomenal." Laws says he has everything from ten-dollar bottles to some that are worth three to four thousand dollars; he thinks he's got about seven hundred different whiskies, but renovations on his home were ongoing when we spoke so a lot of them were stashed away in boxes. About twenty or thirty of his bottles are at the distillery, to be used in tastings.

Laws doesn't buy whiskey casually, and he hasn't embarked on what I consider one of the most exciting craft distilling projects ever undertaken casually, either. The first spirit run took place on July 11, 2011, but he'd been working actively on the project for five years by then, and it had been percolating for long before that. The primary motivation was his love of whiskey, but not far behind that was a desire to be making it. Without both those things, it's inconceivable that he would have made such a major investment and done it in a way that would guarantee not a penny of return until late summer 2014, when his first whiskey—A.D. Laws Four-Grain Bourbon—will be released. The typical bourbon mashbill is corn, malted barley to facilitate the starch-to-sugar conversion, and a small amount of rye or wheat for flavor, but rarely both. Tuthilltown makes a four-grain bourbon under its Hudson label, Koval has one, and Labrot & Graham, an excellent Kentucky whiskey maker, distilled one batch of four-grain bourbon in 1999 and released it under the Woodford Reserve Master's Collection label in 2005 and 2006.

Even this far into the project, much remains undecided, and many things have changed. Given Laws's background in finance and the many years he spent thinking about this endeavor, it was a surprise to find that he's had to make radical adjustments so early in the process. When I asked if there'd been any surprises he replied, "The whole thing is big surprises! In terms of production, we're 50 percent ahead of our original plan. We've had to accelerate capital projects because we're going to run out of room for barrels. We're putting every dollar we can into laying whiskey down now. If it goes down early you have more flexibility. The more that goes down early, the more potential aging projects you can do in the future. We have not been shy about making additional investments to make it better, more efficient, and easier down the road."

Unlike craft distillers who start out on a homemade contraption and slowly work their way up to top-of-the-line equipment—usually from Carl, Kothe, Holstein, or Vendome—Laws had the money and the knowledge to build a distillery capable of producing significant quantities of whiskey, the barrels to age it in, and the space to store those barrels. Many in the industry have had to cobble together the necessary infrastructure as they've grown; others have had to completely rebuild or move to a new facility. By the time Norris joined Laws, the distillery was operational. It was designed with efficiency in mind so that one man can run it alone, but that also limits what can be done. As Norris says, however, this is just the beginning. "We have three or four tiers mapped out on how to expand. We've got financial trigger points that say when we hit this we can do that. As we grow, things will be segmented, and we'll have a dedicated stillman, a dedicated fermentation guy."

LAWS WHISKEY HOUSE was the only one of the half dozen or so start-ups I visited that was able to pour money into production with the knowledge that there wouldn't be a penny of return for several years. No matter how good a distiller Norris is, this is still an extremely risky proposition. By the time the distillery comes out with a product, it will have invested millions of dollars and will be sitting on several thousand fifty-three-gallon barrels of whiskey. Conceptually, everything seems right, and my gut tells me the spirits will be top notch and that they will be well received. Still, it's a brave and laudable leap of faith.

"On paper," says Norris, who spends the first hour with a prospective consulting client trying to talk him out of his or her dream, "you'd have to be insane to open a distillery. It's such a gamble. I really feel for everybody that's willy-nilly throwing their hats in the ring because there are going to be a lot of people who lose it all because they're not qualified to be in the game. They don't have the experience, they're too cheap to hire the people who do have the experience, or they're using half-

assed homemade equipment. Al's doing it for the right reasons, and he understands the rewards."

For his part, Laws says, "We're doing this because we want to make whiskey. The business part will come. I have a good idea of what I want to accomplish."

The whiskies they plan to bottle cover what Norris refers to as the "mother grains" of American whiskies. "We're going to do a corn whiskey, a rye whiskey, a barley whiskey, and a wheat whiskey, and we're doing a four-grain bourbon, which is all of those grains as one whiskey. Those are the whiskies that Americans made, and we want to do one of each."

The bourbon will be released first, and Norris is encouraged by how the spirit is maturing. "It has to have some grip on it so it can hold up to the barrel, but it's already got all this great flavor. The danger might be that it's almost too balanced. In the beginning my heads cuts were too big so it was overly smooth and I was afraid it was going to lose character, so I reeled the heads cut back so you get that slight astringent suck on the tongue. It's got a little bit of teeth so it can sit in the barrels longer, meaning two to five years—if all of this is done properly, it can go to possibly six or eight years, maybe more. I don't know if I would try that."

Whiskey is many things for Laws, including his dreams for the future. "Where I'd rather be," he says, "is dumping bags of grain. I'd rather do that than go to the office every day." Norris is going through a similar thought process, but ironically his path could lead him away from making whiskey. "You've got to have an exit strategy," he says. "If I can get to where I'm financially okay, if I can sell a few knives a year—if I do

OPPOSITE: Jake Norris (center) and Laws Whiskey House coworkers Aleksandr Alexander (left) and Stephen Julander (right).

make a great name I can sell them for about $2,000 apiece—I intend to do that at some point. I'm very, very passionate about food and cooking. As a result I'm kind of a groupie of chefs in town. Most of them like whiskey so it's mutual, and I wanted to make the knives that I couldn't afford. I'm not going to spend three grand on a knife! That's a lot of money. But I want that knife because I know what it is, and I know what it does. When I really have a profound respect for something, I have to participate in it."

This seems to perfectly reflect Al Laws's attitude. "Everyone wants to make whiskey," he says. "Not because they like it, but because they hear whiskey's hot now. If you don't like it, don't make it! Whiskey is more than just a drink, there's a higher impact to really great whiskey. It's got a psychic value that's not in other spirits. We're doing this because we love whiskey. We're doing it for ourselves."

Two Seattle-area distilleries are also taking the more difficult but more righteous path. **WOODINVILLE WHISKEY CO.** was founded by Brett Carlile, who was in sales, and Orlin Sorensen, who was a pilot until the faltering economy led him to create a web-based business dedicated to "natural vision improvement." The two had been friends since high school and, serendipitously, each of them came across articles about craft distilling and were very intrigued. They decided to go for it when, as Sorensen says, "The feeling of not doing it was outweighing all the commonsense considerations."

One of the smartest things they did early on was hire Dave Pickerell as a consultant (see Chapter 2). "We knew basic distilling principles," says Sorensen, "but we felt to just hope that it would turn out good in four to six years wasn't a good idea." Pickerell worked with them to develop a recipe, and he turned them to the rye side. Their two flagship products will be a 100 percent rye (one of only a handful made in this country) and a bourbon with a very high percentage of rye in the mashbill. The typical bourbon might have 12 to 15 percent rye at most; Woodinville's is over 30 percent. About three-quarters of its whiskey production goes into fifty-three-gallon barrels, and the rest goes into eight-gallon barrels for its Microbarreled Collection. (A tiny amount of a second, even-higher-rye bourbon is put away in special casks that have been seasoned for thirty-six months, pre-toasted, and lightly charred. They don't talk about this whisky, and I'm going to do my best not to think about it again for several years so that I don't drive myself crazy with anticipation.)

The still runs every day, year-round. A typical workday lasts thirteen to fourteen hours, starting at five-thirty in the morning. In addition to the bourbon and rye, Woodinville also makes a vodka, which has been the company's primary source of revenue since opening in 2010, and a couple of white whiskies. When

Carlile and Sorensen are making vodka or white dog, they're not making whiskey for aging, so although the revenue is a necessity, and their bottled clear spirits have helped establish their brand in the marketplace, they have to be careful not to lose sight of their goal, which is to make great bourbon and rye. "What we don't make today," says Sorensen, "we won't have in four to six years. So the still runs." He also says they've sold only 15 percent of what they've made in their first three years in business. In other industries this would not be sustainable, but for a distiller there's no better investment.

The microbarreled bourbon and rye are the best whiskies I've tasted to come from small barrels. They still show a bit of the spiky tannins I find problematic, but the bourbon has a beautiful fruitiness, and the rye handles the wood extremely well. Based on Woodinville's small-barrel-aged whiskies, I suspect the mature, big-barrel releases—which should start to come out in 2015—will stand up to anything of comparable age coming out of Kentucky, and I expect the rye to blow a lot of industrially made ryes away. As Sorensen says, "We want to be the best and oldest craft whiskey on the market and have the volume to support the brand."

This probably puts them squarely in the crosshairs of some large liquor company looking to acquire a craft whiskeymaker. I wouldn't begrudge Sorensen and Carlile the return on their investment, but I hope they can hold out at least long enough for me to see that ultra-premium, high-rye bourbon come to market. Oops! I said I wasn't going to think about that.

OPPOSITE: Micah Nutt (left) and Jason Parker (right), partners at Seattle's Copperworks Distilling Company.

Jason Parker is a Kentucky native, but it was not a straight line to the founding of another Seattle-area distillery, **COPPERWORKS DISTILLING COMPANY**, one of the most impressive new craft distilleries in America. Jason became a beverage professional in 1989, when he was hired as the first brewer at Pike Place Brewing, in Seattle's famed Pike Place Market. He later helped open Fish Brewing Company, in Olympia, Washington, was cellerman at Redhook Ale Brewery, and spent seven years as brewmaster at Pyramid. So he's got the fermentation part down. In 2000, he left Pyramid and spent the next thirteen years as a business analyst, seven of those with the Gates Foundation. So he's well rounded. But, even with his BS in chemistry, opening a distillery was not an obvious career move.

"On a visit to see my parents in Kentucky about four years ago," says Parker, "I walked into Corsair's little plant in Bowling Green [see Chapter 5]. They'd just built it, and they had a three-barrel still—that's the size of the first kettle we had at Pike Place. They were just experimenting. They didn't have answers, just the passion. I knew some of the answers in terms of production and fermentation; what I didn't know was distillation. I spent a year convincing my girlfriend it wasn't a bad idea. I spent another year with Dry Fly [see Chapter 5] and up in Snohomish with Glen Mac Donald [owner of Mac Donald Distillery], and finally met with my business partner, Micah Nutt—I've known him for twenty-two years—and he wanted to be an investor. It's just the two of us, which is really nice."

Parker entered the craft brewing industry at roughly the stage that most people say craft distilling is at today, which gives him a unique perspective. Several of the small distilleries I visited were crammed to the gills with equipment and inventory; several others were in the process of expanding. Copperworks was designed to avoid that seeming inevitability. "You build your first brewery, and then you tear it out while you're trying to keep production," says Parker. You build your second brewery; you tear *it* out, and you build a new tank farm and you move things around. Then you build your third brewery, all in the same place for no reason other than that you didn't have the foresight or the money to build it right the first time."

Building it right to begin with obviously requires a large up-front investment, though it's certainly more efficient and probably a lot more sustainable than starting small and expanding to meet demand. Given his location, which is in the heart of a Seattle waterfront in the midst of a massive upgrade, and the importance of foot traffic in a state where it's legal for a distillery to sell direct, it's understandable that Parker would want to avoid the disruptions of remodeling. When I saw the seven-thousand-square-foot space, the equipment hadn't yet arrived, but it was easy to imagine a crowd of people gazing down at the four stills as they toured the facility. What was less easy for me to imagine was how such a big project was executed. "I kind of didn't want to quit my day job at the Gates Foundation," Parker says. "It was a pretty good gig. I'd been doing it for seven years, and I loved it there. And people there liked me, so I put the bar really high: I've got to raise a lot of money, I've got to be in the Pike Place Market or on the Seattle Waterfront, and I've got to build it right. I figured that all three of those would fail, and I was sure that at least two would fail. But I didn't think there was any possibility that all three would hit. But they did, so I had to give notice."

Parker remembered what it was like to brew in Pike Place Market, and that led him to his location. "I learned that this is a wonderful area to be in business," he says. "You get two things you don't get anywhere else: you get people coming by who have money and have time, and they want to learn. Everywhere else, in neighborhoods like Capital Hill and Queen Anne, you just have people coming by shopping. Here it's a fresh bunch of people every day." It's also right across the street from Seattle Steam Company, so Copperworks will be able to use a very local heat source to power its stills.

The stills were made in Scotland, by Forsyths. The largest, a fifteen-foot-tall, 4,000-liter (1,057-gallon) wash still, weighs close to three tons. The spirit still holds 2,650 liters (700 gallons), and the spirit can be directed through the long neck for whiskey or up a column with twenty-two plates to make a neutral grain spirit. Parker might bottle a little of that as vodka, but most of it will be used for gin, which will be produced in a 250-liter (66-gallon) still that is a replica of an early-nineteenth-century gin still from London. The mash will be all malt, and it will be made off-site at Elysian Brew-

ery, which has a big, new facility less than five miles south of Copperworks, and fermented in three large stainless steel tanks at the distillery. The output from all this equipment should be about two 53-gallon barrels of whiskey a day. At that rate it will take less than a year to fill the two-thousand-square-foot barrel storage area. What happens at that point depends on whether the state liquor control board brings its regulation, which requires barrels to be stored "in contiguous sight of the distillery," in line with federal regulations, which allow barrel aging within ten miles of the distillery. If not, barrels will have to be stacked wherever space can be found.

Despite his extremely systematic approach, it's clear that Parker also has an adventuresome streak. "I can have different brewers come in, and we can have whiskies made from all these different malt bills," he says. "And I'm really looking forward to experimenting with different woods and with small barrels. Bartenders here have become pretty skeptical of anything that's not aged, and anything that's aged in small barrels, and anything that's aged less than four years. But I think we can probably do what Stranahan's is doing. They make wonderful, clear, clean wash—sanitary fermentation, no bacteria—and age it two years. My opinion is that their two-year-old is better than their three-year-old. It has more malt. It has more springiness to it. When you get to the three-year, it's still good, but it's not as exciting. Stranahan's is my model, but one of the big things I'm doing differently is their stills have a tiny column on top of a big-shouldered pot, and I just know what you can get out of a true Scottish whiskey still."

OPPOSITE: The stills at Copperworks were made
by Forsyths in Scotland.

EPILOGUE

Further proof, not that more was needed, of the volatility of craft distilling came as we were putting the finishing touches on this book. Clear Creek Distillery (see Chapter 4), one of the oldest and best craft distillers in the country, was sold to Hood River Distillers. The "distillers" part of the latter company's name hasn't been true since the 1960s, when Hood River became a bottler and marketer of product made elsewhere. Its best-known brand is probably Pendleton, a Canadian whiskey it buys and bottles. The sale is either good news, if it means Hood River wants to make what it sells, or terrible news, if it means accountants will start making Clear Creek's production decisions. Some of my best friends are accountants, but I'd rather have Stephen McCarthy, with his long experience distilling eaux de vie, whiskies, brandies, and liqueurs, deciding what to make and how to make it. McCarthy will stay on as an "adviser and spokesman," so there's hope.

At around the same time as the Clear Creek sale, Proximo released another Colorado product to complement its Stranahan's Colorado Whiskey (see Chapter 9). Tincup American Whiskey is reportedly distilled in Indiana and, according to the company's website, "cut with pure Rocky Mountain water." The Tincup website is full of Colorado references, the label actually says "Tincup, Colorado," and the face of the brand is Jess Graber, one of the founders of Stranahan's. It's clear what Proximo is trying to convey. As a business strategy I suppose it makes sense. If Proximo thinks it can capitalize on local patriotism and move buyers of inexpensive whiskey from one of the major brands to one of its own, it would be stupid not to do so. And if Proximo thinks other Colorado products are cannibalizing sales from Stranahan's, as brand ambassador Kristin Forsch told me, of course it should fight back. But there's definitely the potential for Tincup to have a major negative impact on distillers in the state who are actually making what they sell and not just bottling an industrial product. A craft distiller would have a very hard time putting out a bottle of whiskey it made from grain to bottle at a suggested retail price of $27.99. I have nothing against competition, but current labeling rules allow a level of deception that strikes me as unfair. A level playing field would require a much clearer indication of where a spirit is distilled than is presently required.

Meanwhile, some of the largest industrial liquor companies have made well-financed forays into craft, or at least craft-washing. Less than a month after Tincup was launched, Diageo (the world's largest spirits maker) released the first two products bottled by the Orphan Barrel Whiskey Distilling Company. The penultimate word in that company's name is as misleading as the "Colorado" on Tincup's label because it's a bottler, not a distiller. The first two Orphan Barrel bourbons, Barterhouse and Old Blowhard, come from "found" whiskies made

by Bernheim; the former is a twenty-year-old, the latter is a twenty-six-year-old. By all accounts they are very good bourbons, but the Barterhouse label has "well crafted quality" at the top and "always crafted to the highest standards" at the bottom. Orphan Barrel back labels brag that "we take craft and quality seriously" and that every whiskey is "hand bottled." Instead of disclosing where the spirit was distilled or who actually made it, there's a line for "curator name," which makes perfect sense given the vogue for attaching that sobriquet to all manner of positions well outside the cultural sphere. As if "sommelier" wasn't pretentious enough, high-end restaurants now have wine curators; clothing stores don't display their wares, they curate them; coffee shops don't just roast their beans, they curate their selections.

And three major Kentucky players have invested heavily in small downtown Louisville distilleries. Evan Williams, the second-largest bourbon brand (Jim Beam, which was acquired at the beginning of 2014 by Japanese drinks giant Suntory for $16 billion, is number one), reportedly spent $10.5 million on its Evan Williams Bourbon Experience, which includes what the company is calling an "artisanal distillery." Michter's, a venerable whiskey name that went belly-up in the late 1980s, was revived as a bottler in the mid-1990s, and has been having its spirits made at other plants, now has two multimillion-dollar projects underway. In December 2013, Michter's hired Pamela Heilmann, previously distillery manager at Jim Beam's Booker Noe Distillery, to run its $10.9 million factory in Shively, Kentucky, a suburb of Louisville. The company is also refurbishing a downtown building built in the 1870s to house its tourist distillery/gift shop. Angel's Envy, founded by former Brown-Forman master distiller Lincoln Henderson (sadly, Henderson died September 10, 2013), is transforming a dilapidated factory complex into a $12 million distillery. The company, which currently buys whiskey, finishes it and bottles it, hopes to begin distilling in December 2014.

Sure, major corporations love to capitalize on the hard work of others, and if they're on the ball at all they'll ride the latest trend as far as it will take them. But the millions being invested in the craft message, even if it smacks of crass appropriation, could also benefit smaller producers. None of this—not the bad, not the good—would have been possible without the growth of craft distilling. It turns out that we love to see things actually being made. We like interacting with the people who create high-quality products. And when it comes to the stuff we put in our mouths, we're increasingly curious about where it came from, how it was put together, why certain decisions were made, and what the impacts of those decisions will be on others. And that strikes me as very good news.

NOTES

INTRODUCTION

Page XVIII, ". . . quadruple over the next ten years." Coppersea Distilling, "Spreading the News . . .," Coppersea.com, July 2, 2012, http://www .coppersea.com/2012/07/02/spreading-the-news/.

CHAPTER 1

Page 2, ". . . It sounds like the same thing." Interview with Chip Tate, June 19, 2012.

Page 11, ". . . 'handmade' on his label." Beverage Dynamics, beverage dynamics.com, March/April 2011.

Page 13, ". . . exposure to gamma rays." William J. Broad, "Useful Mutants, Bred with Radiation," *The New York Times*, August 28, 2007, http://www.nytimes.com/2007/08/28/science/28crop.html.

Page 13, ". . . owners of Jose Cuervo, among other brands." "William Grant & Sons Take on Hudson Whiskey Range," GrantUSA.com (William Grant & Sons website), June 4, 2010, http://www.grantusa.com/index .php?q=press&prid=12; Paula Moore, "Proximo Spirits Buys Strana-han's Colorado Whiskey," *Denver Business Journal*, December 23, 2010, in BizJournals.com, http://www.bizjournals.com/denver/news/2010/12/23 /stranahans.html.

Page 14, ". . . other 'craft' whiskies—to Chattanooga." Joe Ledbetter, "Chattanooga Whiskey—The Return," Kickstarter.com, accessed March 3, 2014, http://www.kickstarter.com/projects/joeledbetter /chattanooga-whiskey-the-return; Andy Sher and Ellis Smith, "Chattanooga Whiskey Can't Be Made in Chattanooga Due to Prohibition-Era Laws," *Chattanooga Times Free Press*, October 9, 2012, http://www .timesfreepress.com/news/2012/oct/09/chattanooga-whiskey-wars-overtake-hamilton-county/.

Page 16, ". . . had turned to dollar signs." Interview with Dan Garrison, June 18, 2012.

Page 20, ". . . the relationship between brewing and distilling." Interview with Mark McDavid and T.J Miller, June 27, 2012.

Page 21, ". . . three small-barrel whiskies." Ranger Creek Brewing & Distilling, "Ranger Creek *Small-Caliber Series*," DrinkRangerCreek.com, http://www.drinkrangercreek.com/whiskey/small-caliber-series/.

CHAPTER 2

Page 26, ". . . gristmill in Gardiner, New York." Alan Snel, "Gardiner Mill's New Owner Talks Bed-and-Breakfast," *The Times Herald-Record*, April 28, 2001, http://www.recordonline.com/apps/pbcs.dll /article?AID=/20010428/NEWS/304289993.

Page 26, ". . . to pay the bills." "Bunks in the Gunks," *Expedition News*, June 2002, http://expeditionnews.com/Archives/EN0206.html.

Page 26, ". . . for larger producers." Paul Adams, "Whiskey's Hudson Valley Revival," *The New York Times*, June 21, 2006, http://www.nytimes .com/2006/06/21/dining/21distill.html.

Page 26, ". . . at his discretion." Gunks.com.

Page 27, ". . . feeding the apples to the pigs." Interview with Ralph Erenzo, June 25, 2012.

Page 39, ". . . bringing a new taste to market." Interview with Dave Pickerell, April 7, 2013.

CHAPTER 3

Page 48, ". . . Tribeca Film Festival." *The Fish Miracle Sky (When Fishes Cry, the Miracle, Closer to the Sky)*, directed by George Rácz, New York, 2006; information at TribecaFilm.com, http://tribecafilm.com/filmguide /archive/512d04061c7d76e046002668-fish-miracle-sky-when-fis.

Page 49, ". . . very lucky in my life—every time." Interview with George Rácz, August 1, 2012.

Page 59, ". . . Who needs a high-end architect?" Interview with Colin Keegan, July 30, 2012.

CHAPTER 4

Page 67, ". . . everything else from Europe that I could eat or drink." Interview with Stephen McCarthy, August 8, 2012.

Page 74, ". . . boxes of cornflakes." Archer Daniels Midland Company, "Overview," ADM.com, accessed March 3, 2014, http://www.adm.com /company/Documents/ADM Overview.pdf.

CHAPTER 5

Page 85, ". . . to taste the rye or the wheat." Interview with Sonat Birnecker Hart and Robert Birnecker, November 29, 2012.

Page 88, ". . . but we're working on it." Interview with Matt Strickland, November 30, 2012.

Page 91, ". . . I can make a living at it, too." Interview with Clay Smith, December 1, 2012.

Page 94, ". . . it's made in Washington." Interview with Don Poffenroth, September 21, 2012.

CHAPTER 6

Page 101, ". . . I wandered in through the door." Interview with Lance Winters and Ellie Winters, August 6, 2012.

Page 124, ". . . powdered toasted-cumin seed on top." Interview with Litty Mathew, August 13, 2012.

Page 129, ". . . blow up the town with our stills." Interview with Mo Heck and Al Heck, September 20, 2012.

CHAPTER 7

Page 138, ". . . we never bought grapes out of Fresno." Interview with Ansley Coale, August 3, 2012.

Page 146, ". . . it's really twenty-five-plus years." Interview with Dan Farber, August 11, 2012.

CHAPTER 8

Page 161, ". . . graduate student to unravel." Associated Press, "Navy Decides Sailors May Not Have Beards," *The New York Times*, December 15, 1984, http://www.nytimes.com/1984/12/15/us/navy-decides-sailors-may-not-have-beards.html.

Page 161, ". . . roughly $40 million." David Mielach, "The Brewery That Brought Beer Back to Brooklyn," *Business News Daily*, March 18, 2012, http://www.businessnewsdaily.com/2205-brooklyn-brewery-story.html.

Page 163, ". . . let's stop by The Shanty.' " Interview with Allen Katz, June 22, 2012.

Page 167, ". . . the 'richer Dutch style.' " David Wondrich, *Imbibe!*, New York: Perigee, 2007.

Page 169, ". . . seized with a cough." T.A. Atchison, "Alcohol and Its Effects," *Memphis Medical Monthly*, vol. 10: 1890, Google Books, accessed March 3, 2014, http://books.google.com/.

Page 169, ". . . Maryland Rock and Rye." Eric Felten, "A Cocktail for What Ails You," *The Wall Street Journal*, June 6, 2009, http://online.wsj.com/article/SB10001424052970204456604574207740025188798.html.

Page 172, ". . . a curiosity about moonshine." Interview with Colin Spoelman, June 23, 2012.

Page 180, ". . . and a gardener and a cook." Interview with Daric Schlesselman, June 24, 2012.

CHAPTER 9

Page 187, ". . . it was my priority." Interview with Jake Norris, September 25, 2012.

Page 189, ". . . so people wouldn't get confused." Interview with Kristin Forsch and Rob Dietrich, September 24, 2012.

Page 195, ". . . Jacob's open mouth." Tony Norris, "A Letter from Home," *News*, TonyNorris.com, May 18, 2006, http://tonynorris.com /tonynorris_news.html.

Page 199, ". . . and easier down the road." Interview with Al Laws, March 17, 2013.

Page 191 ". . . model will fall apart." Janet Patton, "The Spirit of Kentucky: Bourbon Is More of a Commodity Than Many Realize," *Lexington Herald-Leader* (Kentucky), December 7, 2013, http://www.kentucky .com/2013/12/07/2976234/the-spirit-of-kentucky-bourbon.html.

Page 203, ". . . all the commensense considerations." Quotations from Orlin Sorensen from interview, September 20, 2012.

Page 206, ". . . which is really nice." Interview with Jason Parker, September 19, 2012.

EPILOGUE

Page 211, ". . . sold to Hood River Distillers." Malia Spencer, "Hood River Distillers Buys Oregon Whiskey Maker," *Portland Business Journal*, January 24, 2014, in BizJournals.com, http://www.bizjournals.com /portland/blog/2014/01/hood-river-distillers-buying-clear.html.

Page 213, ". . . a twenty-six-year-old." http://photos.prnewswire.com/featured
/prnthumbnew/20140211/NY63014.

Page 213, ". . . an 'artisanal distillery.' " Janet Patton, "Beam Inc. to Be
Acquired by Japan's Suntory in Deal Worth $16 Billion," *Lexington
Herald-Leader* (Kentucky), January 13, 2014, http://www.kentucky
.com/2014/01/13/3031681/beam-inc-to-be-acquired-by-japanese.html.

Page 213, ". . . a suburb of Louisville." "Distiller Pamela Heilmann Joins
Michter's Distillery," Press Release, November 19, 2013, PRNewswire
.com, http://www.prnewswire.com/news-releases/distiller-pamela-
heilmann-joins-michters-distillery-232502101.html

Page 214, ". . . a $12 million distillery." Fred Minnick, "Angel's Envy
Distillery Breaks Ground," *WhiskyAdvocate.com*, July 11, 2013, http://
whiskyadvocate.com/whisky/2013/07/11/angels-envy-distillery-breaks-
ground/.

GLOSSARY

ACETOBACTERIA Creates vinegar by converting alcohol into acetic acid. This is not desirable in fermentation for distillation.

ALEMBIC STILL Early pot still. It continues to be used in Cognac and by a few brandy makers in the United States.

AMARO (PLURAL: AMARI) A bitter digestif, traditionally from Italy, usually made with a grape-spirit base infused with any number of herbs, spices, barks, flowers, and citrus peels.

ANGELS' SHARE Alcohol that evaporates from whiskey stored in wood barrels. In humid climates more alcohol evaporates than water, resulting in a lower-proof spirit; in less humid climates, more water is lost and the concentration of alcohol rises.

ARMAGNAC Brandy produced in Gascony, France. Unlike Cognac, it's distilled only once.

BATCH DISTILLATION Fermented mash is placed in the still, and the entire volume is processed. (See *Continuous distillation*.)

BITTERS Aromatic flavoring made from plants, seeds, herbs, barks, and/or roots infused in distilled spirits (generally very high proof). Bitters are a key ingredient in many cocktails (e.g., Manhattan, Sazerac, Old Fashioned).

BOURBON Whiskey made in the United States from a fermented mash of not less than 51 percent corn and stored in charred new oak containers.

BRANDY Spirit made from fermented fruit or fruit juice.

BRIX Measure of the sugar content of fruit and therefore of its potential alcohol.

BUBBLE CUP Used in the column to interrupt the flow of alcohol vapor, thus enriching the spirit by creating additional reflux.

CALVADOS Apple brandy produced in Lower Normandy, France.

CARTER HEAD Perforated botanicals basket placed in the column or between the column and the condenser in a still. Alcohol vapor passes through the botanicals and extracts flavor compounds. It's used in production of gin, absinthe, and other spirits. The process yields more delicate flavors than boiling botanicals in the still or steeping them in the alcohol.

CHAI French for "warehouse."

CHAR Measure of how much a barrel is flame-treated (that is, burned). Light char tends to impart spice and fruit; dark char, vanilla. (See *Toast.*)

COGNAC Grape brandy produced in the Cognac region of France. It's generally distilled twice.

COLUMN STILL (COFFEY STILL) Designed for continuous distillation. The process is more efficient, but it makes a less-flavorful spirit.

CONTINUOUS DISTILLATION Fermented mash is put into the still at the same rate as spirit is withdrawn.

CORN WHISKEY Made from a fermented mash of not less than 80 percent corn. (Note that the minimum requirement for bourbon is 51 percent.) It can't be stored in or treated with new or charred oak. It's sometimes referred to, as "legal moonshine."

CUTS During pot still distillation the first spirit that comes off the still (heads) contains unpleasant and toxic compounds, including methanol. The middle cut, called the "hearts," is primarily ethanol. The final cut, or "tails," occurs when desirable flavors are no longer being produced.

EAU DE VIE Clear, unaged brandy made from fruits other than grapes. (Hans Reisetbauer makes one from carrots, but that's more than unusual.) Eau de vie is usually made with the solids in the still, requiring the mash to be stirred constantly to avoid scorching. It's very aromatic.

FEINTS See *Tails.*

FUSEL OILS Low-boiling compounds that come off the still late in the second distillation. These are flavorful but unpleasant in large quantities. (See *Tails.*)

GIN Spirit—usually grain—flavored with botanicals, primarily juniper berries. Other ones might include coriander, citrus peel, angelica, cassia, anise, fennel, gingerroot, and almond.

GRAIN NEUTRAL SPIRIT See *Neutral grain spirit.*

GRAPPA Brandy made from leftover stems, seeds, and skins after grapes are pressed for wine.

HEADS Early-boiling compounds such as methanol and acetone. Once the distiller determines these are no longer coming off the still, the middle cut (heart, spirit run) is collected for bottling or aging.

HEART Middle "cut" in pot still distillation. The primary alcohol collected is ethanol. When to begin and end this cut is critical for flavor but also because the heart cut is what a company can bottle and sell.

LIQUEUR Any spirit flavored with fruits or plants and containing not less than 2.5 percent sugar by weight.

LOW WINES Low-proof spirit collected after a first distillation in a wash still.

MALT/MALTING Sprouting of a grain (usually barley) in order to convert its starches into fermentable sugars. Sprouting is arrested with heat.

MASH Milled grain and water. Once fermented, it's called "wash" (or "beer," but it has no carbonation or—usually—hops).

MASH BILL Specific grain recipe that goes into the mash (e.g., a bourbon might be 70 percent corn, 20 percent rye, and 10 percent malt). The term is sometimes spelled as one word.

MASH TUN Vessel for cooking mash in preparation for fermentation.

MOONSHINE Illegally made, untaxed spirit made on a still not registered with the Alcohol and Tobacco Tax and Trade Bureau (TTB).

NEUTRAL GRAIN SPIRIT Spirit distilled from a fermented mash of grain to "at or above" 95 percent alcohol by volume (190 proof).

NEW MAKE Unaged and uncut whiskey straight off the still.

PEAT Traditional fuel for drying malt in Scotland. Imparts smoky flavors to whiskies, particularly those from Islay, Orkney, and Campbelltown.

PLATES Adjustable metal disks inserted at intervals in the column of the still to interrupt vapors and enrich spirit (see *Bubble cup*). These allow greater control during distillation.

POMACE Residue of winemaking. (See *Grappa*.)

POT STILL Batch-process still, usually copper, usually fat and round with a long neck that gradually narrows to the condenser. It can be heated by direct fire (gas, coal, wood, peat) or with steam running in coils inside the still.

PROHIBITION The Noble Experiment to ban alcohol, which lasted from 1920 to 1933. It's now considered a failure. After repeal, each state was allowed to draft its own liquor laws. (Mississippi did not repeal its state prohibition until 1966.) Craft distillers have had to work hard to change various statutes to make the industry viable.

PROOF A measure of alcohol's strength at 60 degrees Fahrenheit. In the United States, proof is twice the percentage by volume of alcohol. (For example, 80 proof is 40 percent alcohol by volume.)

REFLUX Process of alcohol vapors condensing and returning to be reheated and revaporized. Still construction, neck length, bubble-cups, and plates all impact reflux.

RICKHOUSE Warehouse where barrels of whiskey are stored for aging. The term is sometimes written as two words.

RUM Spirits distilled from the fermented juice of sugarcane, sugarcane syrup, sugar cane molasses, or other sugarcane by-products.

RYE Whiskey made in the United States from a fermented mash of not less than 51 percent rye and stored in charred new oak containers.

SECOND DISTILLATION Also called "spirit run"; low wines are heated, and the most volatile (early boiling) compounds come off first (see *Heads*). The next fraction is mostly ethanol (see *Heart*). The final part is full of flavor, but not all those flavors are desirable (see *Tails*).

SINGLE MALT Whisky produced from only water and malted barley at a single distillery by batch distillation in pot stills.

STILL Distilling apparatus consisting of a vessel in which the liquid is heated until it vaporizes and a cooling device in which the vapor is condensed. It's often made of copper for its sulfur-neutralizing properties.

STRAIGHT WHISKEY A whiskey that's been stored in charred new oak containers for two years or more. TTB rules allow straight whiskies to be mixtures of like types provided that all the whiskies are made in the same state.

TAILS Final fraction of spirit distillation. Tails are flavorful, but they can become unpleasant. Long aging in wood can mitigate negative effect of tails. Unaged spirits require more rigorous tails cuts.

TEQUILA Agave spirit made in specific areas of Mexico using blue agave (*Agave tequilana Weber var. azul*).

TOAST Degree and duration of heating applied to a wood barrel in order to transform its structure (without applying flame directly to the wood; see *Char*). It's more common in wine than spirits.

TTB Alcohol and Tobacco Tax and Trade Bureau. Tasked with collecting federal excise taxes on alcohol and assuring compliance with federal alcohol permitting, labeling, and marketing requirements. The bureau itself seems to be overtaxed.

VODKA Neutral spirits distilled or treated after distillation with charcoal or other materials so as to be without distinctive character, aroma, taste, or color. (In order to be vodka, it must be distilled to at least 190 proof. Other countries have different rules.)

WASH When the mash has finished fermenting, it's called "wash" (also "distiller's beer").

WASH STILL In batch distillation, this is the first still. Wash is transformed into low wines, which are then distilled to high proof in the spirit still.

WASH TUN Vessel for fermenting mash.

WHISKEY/WHISKY Spelled without the *e* in Scotland, Canada, and Japan; with the *e* just about everywhere else.

WHITE DOG/WHITE WHISKEY Unaged whiskey diluted to bottling strength. It's often inaccurately called "moonshine."

ACKNOWLEDGMENTS

I couldn't have written one word if not for Norma Cross, the first alchemist I knew, and still my favorite. Thanks, Mom. I also couldn't have done it without the support and generosity of Melissa Allison and David Turim; Merik, Macey, Maddie, Mike, and Sariya Jarasviroj Brown; Dan Burns; Chase, Will, Steve, and Nicole Carter; Judith and Guy Cross; Taj, Camille, and Jason Cross; Jay and Marty Feldman; Dan Fredman; Barbara and Robert Koffsky; Sarah McCarthy; Wyatt, Jamie, and Shawn Meade; David Millman; Alan Myerson; Tom Rapp, Toshi Sakihara, and everyone at Cochineal Restaurant; Tami Spector and Rachel Crawford.

I owe a huge debt to all the distillers who shared with me who they are, what they do, and—best of all—what they make. Even those who are not mentioned by name were crucial to my understanding of what it means to be a craft distiller. Many more of them deserved to be written about; my one consolation is that I know they now will be. As for those who *are* mentioned, any errors or omissions are mine and mine alone. Mostly, to paraphrase Yogi Berra, thank you for making this book necessary.

Finally, a big thank you to Carlo DeVito for giving me the opportunity to spend time with these amazing people, and an even bigger thank you to my editor, Diane Abrams, for achieving the nearly impossible task of keeping me (almost) on schedule.

CREDITS

INDEX